Praise

'I devoured the book. Its natural writing style, practical activities and golden questions have made me examine my leadership through a new lens. So much is possible when you anticipate success and work accordingly.'
   —**Andrea Saunders**, Finance Director

'As Lynn suggests in the book, I worked through my thoughts just before a meeting I was nervous about and not looking forward to. I went in with energy and a positive agenda and – big win – a better relationship with the person I was meeting. Goal achieved – this works!'
   —**Emma Beckley**, Director, Adobe

'This book is like a gym session for your thoughts. The Future You exercises are some of the most powerful I have ever done in my leadership career.'
   —**Jane Harding**, Product Owner, wealth and asset management

'One of the lightbulb moments for me in this book was realising how easily I could replace the inner monologue or "critic" driving my actions. Realising I can change those thoughts and in turn, my degree of influence, without fundamentally having to change who I am is liberating. It's made me more confident and courageous in my conversations.'
   —**Pamela Laing**, Head of HR Organisation Effectiveness, BAE Systems

'Jargon-free, powerful and accessible activities throughout. Every single one of them will improve your leadership.'
   —**Sam Grayston**, strategic leadership coach
      and consultant

'This book is a wonderful and insightful tool for enabling leaders to reach their potential in business and in life. A brilliant read. Lynn Scott's experience and dedication shine through.'
   —**Tamara Gillan**, Founder and CEO, FFinc

Leader Unlocked

How to grow your confidence, influence and impact for leadership success

Lynn Scott

Rethink

First published in Great Britain in 2025
by Rethink Press (www.rethinkpress.com)

Cover image © Shutterstock | Padop

Lightbulb icon courtesy of Adrien Coquet from Noun Project.

Case study icon courtesy of Larea from Noun Project.

To my beautiful sister Sue. Taken too soon.

Contents

Introduction

Let's imagine you and I meet for a drink six months from now. You say, 'Lynn, I want to tell you about all the great things that have happened since I read your book. I feel like a different leader. So much has changed for the better.'

What would you love to tell me?

Answer that question and I'll show you exactly how to get there. This book is your guidebook, compass and map all rolled into one. If there's one thing I've learned over the last twenty-five years working with leaders like you and being a leader myself, it's this: you don't need another 'Ten Traits of an Effective Leader' checklist. You do need to believe from your core that you can do the things you want to do, change the things you want

1

to change and be the leader you yearn to be – the one everyone wants to work with and for – because you can.

You'll only get so far if you're constantly telling yourself, 'I don't have time', or 'I'm not good enough', or 'This won't work'. When one of these thoughts pops into your brain, you're more likely to stick with what you know, the habits and routines familiar to you, even though they might be counterproductive. Your busy brain is taking the congested road well travelled, even though it's time to update the GPS.

I should know. I did this for years. In my first senior leadership role in the travel industry, I worked like a demon, trying to please everyone, but rarely pleasing myself. I struggled to be heard in a room full of swaggering alphas. I loved the work, the chance to travel the world and work with an epic group of people. It still took me two years to feel like I'd earned my seat at the table and realise that the non-stop treadmill I'd been on wasn't where the good stuff happened.

When I left corporate life, I knew there had to be a better way. I've made it my mission to find that better way in the two decades since. The tips you'll get from me in this book have been tried and tested for over twenty years. They work. There's no fluff or nonsense. Some of the activities I invite you to do are simple and easy, but they are just the start.

You'll think bigger and bolder than before, not in a rainbows-and-unicorns way – although I love both a rainbow and a unicorn. You'll dig deep, ask yourself some searching questions and turn some of what you've always believed on its head. You might get squirmy, and that's when you'll know you're in the right place. You don't need to mould yourself into someone else's idea of who you 'should' be because that will make you miserable. Future You is not a perfect, cookie-cutter leader who never puts a foot wrong. That person doesn't exist. You *do* exist, though, in all your unique splendour and glorious imperfection.

This book will uncover that unique splendour and give it a good airing and shake. It'll take you from where you are now to where you want to be because who you are today shapes who you become tomorrow. Every decision you make today is shaping your future.

Please mark the date on your calendar: six months from now. What will you tell me?

- I've been promoted.

- My purpose is clearer.

- I've made a decision.

- I've received a juicy pay rise.

- I'm working less and getting more done.

- My boundaries are stronger.

- I've got my life back.

- I'm speaking up.

- I've stopped trying to please everyone.

- I'm not stuck in the weeds.

Perhaps several of these?

You'll build your belief muscle chapter by chapter as you become crystal-clear on the leader you want to become and take the steps to get there. You'll connect with Future You, blossoming and growing every day as the light gets in. This doesn't mean you're not good enough as you are. You don't need fixing, because you're not broken. You do, however, need to access what you can't see, and I can.

The belief muscle

The next six months

You will achieve several things over the next six months:

1. Learn core beliefs and practices that will build your confidence daily

2. Create time and space where you thought there was none

3. Master the art of dynamic, productive and compelling meetings

4. Visualise and align with the leader you want to become

5. Prime your brain for success daily

6. Chart a path from Current You to Future You

7. Choose your thoughts every day

8. Tame your inner critic by challenging learned beliefs and scripts

9. Learn to navigate emotional responses by regulating your emotions

10. Cultivate authentic confidence from your core

11. Improve your leadership presence through warmth, competence and paying attention to your verbal and nonverbal communication

12. Improve your influence by strengthening your authority, connection and observation

13. Build trust, listen well and be intentional in your choices

14. Build your team's productivity by giving them more responsibility and agency

'Why six months?' you may ask.

I am not making a change-your-life-in-a-week promise because we both know that doesn't work. This book is less 'rush' and more 'reflect and reveal, practise and consolidate'. Every chapter includes practical how-to activities that my clients love because they're powerful and simple. I also share lots of short case studies about clients I've worked with. I hope you'll nod in recognition as you read them and be excited to see how my clients turned things around. You can download the workbook I've prepared at www.effortlessleaders.com/lynn-scott-leader-unlocked. It will help you chart your progress as you work through the activities. You'll also find some additional resources available there. Everything is designed to get you from where you are now to where you want to be in six months in the most brain-friendly, practical, uncomplicated way.

This book provides straight-down-the-line, tried-and-tested guidance and advice that works for my leadership clients every single day. My clients are senior leaders just like you, juggling plates and navigating change, complexity, conflicting priorities and shifting sands. Leaders like you, who want to do their best work because it matters and they care. It's the book I wish I could give my thirty-year-old self and the book I wish I had when I first started coaching leaders back in 2001.

At the end of the book, you'll think differently about who you are, how you lead, what you're truly capable of, what you're ready for and what you choose not to do. You'll also see how to support other people with this. When you flourish, you create a ripple effect that enables others to thrive.

Best of all? You're going to do all this one step at a time. Let's get started.

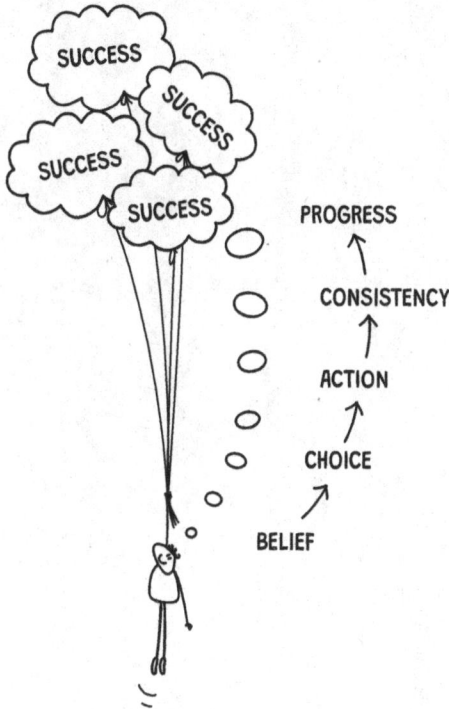

SUCCESS
SUCCESS
SUCCESS
SUCCESS

PROGRESS
↑
CONSISTENCY
↑
ACTION
↑
CHOICE
↗
BELIEF

The success balloon

1
Core Beliefs For Unshakeable Confidence

Your beliefs today and the actions you take based on those beliefs largely dictate what you experience tomorrow, next week, or in six months. Our beliefs shape everything. Generic aphorisms like 'Believe in yourself' and 'Think positive' against a backdrop of beautiful sunsets and palm-fringed beaches change nothing so in this chapter, I will share the six foundational beliefs that are crucial for leadership impact and success. And you'll have an opportunity to put them into practice right away.

Belief 1: I anticipate success in everything I do

Success is whatever *you* want it to be. Whether you want to become a global CEO, work part-time or spend more time with your loved ones (or all of these things), you get to choose. If you anticipate success (rather than avoid failure) in everything you do, guess what? You are more likely to succeed. It's not woo-woo; your brain focuses on what you tell it to focus on. It's your starting point for every decision and action you make. There's a big difference between anticipating success and avoiding failure.

Imagine you have an upcoming meeting with Ms Angry from marketing. If you anticipate success, you'll prepare, think about the outcomes you want and figure out how to get her on board. You'll choose to believe that she's not 'angry' – she simply hates it when people are not on top of the details, and you'll be prepared with said details.

Anticipating success is associated with releasing neurotransmitters such as dopamine, a key player in the brain's reward system. You're more likely to feel optimistic and focused and you'll find different strategies for managing your emotional state. You'll imagine the positive consequences of your actions before they occur. If you focus on avoiding failure, you'll see the meeting with Ms Angry as a potential threat. You'll tell yourself, *She's always angry*, and you'll be hypervigilant, operating from fight-or-flight (survival) mode, which means your executive brain (prefrontal cortex) can't do its best work.

Does anticipating success mean you always succeed? It depends on how you define success and failure and how you think about your experience. Going into anything with the *anticipate-success* belief primes your brain to look for ways to help you be successful. You know how you feel and how you show up when you anticipate success versus how you show up when you anticipate failure. Your energy is different. You look and sound different. People experience you differently, too. Start with Activity 1.

> :bulb: **ACTIVITY 1: Anticipate success right now (5-10 minutes)**
>
> Choose something that's on your mind or your calendar this week. Imagine the activity has happened, and someone says, 'Tell me why you were so successful.' Answer that statement and you'll know exactly what to do now.

There are many other benefits associated with anticipating success, which is also called 'anticipatory utility'. Leaders with high anticipatory utility can motivate their teams by communicating their vision of the future, instilling confidence in their ability to navigate challenges and be successful. This is realistic optimism, not mindless positivity.

Make it a habit to anticipate success daily. I start each day imagining it's 5pm, looking back at the day that I've just had. I ask myself, *Why was today so successful for me?* It encourages me to be clear on:

- What I want to focus on and achieve

- How I want to embody confidence and show up

- How to spend my time

If I miss a day (hey, I'm not perfect), I feel scattered, less on my A-game and I'm more likely to get distracted.

Belief 2: I start before I'm ready

Action leads to confidence, not the other way around, but you need to anticipate success first. Waiting to be more confident is usually an avoidance strategy. You build confidence by doing the thing. Think about all the things you do with ease now that initially terrified you.

This is a challenge for many women in particular. A report by LinkedIn Talent Insights[1] showed that women looking for jobs hold back from applying if they don't meet 100% of the criteria. In comparison, men apply if they meet around 60%. Don't

1   LinkedIn Talent Blog, 'New report: Women apply to fewer jobs than men, but are more likely to get hired', LinkedIn, www.linkedin.com/business/talent/blog/talent-acquisition/how-women-find-jobs-gender-report, accessed 23 September 2024

let a lack of confidence hold you back. Start now, get better later. Version one is always better than version none.

Belief 3: I always have a choice

Some people in organisational life choose to feel powerless or 'done to'. (Notice the word 'choose' – it's deliberate.) You have choices and options – so do the people you work with. They're not always simple or easy, but they're choices nonetheless. When you feel powerless, you lack energy, focus and motivation. You feel stuck, frustrated and resentful. Blaming circumstances or other people for your workplace woes can feel much easier. We call this 'learned helplessness'. Other people become stereotyped persecutors or bad guys – the overly demanding boss or the out-of-touch CEO or the crap executive team.

The truth is, you can't always change your workplace circumstances. You can rarely change other people (unless they want to change), but you can choose how to respond to them, how much energy to give them or how much space to let them take up in your life. The following examples illustrate the difference choosing to change your approach can make.

Example 1: Your team is not delivering. What can *you* choose to influence and change to get a different outcome?

Your team comprises individuals with different skills, hopes and dreams. Ask each of them what they need from you to deliver. Are your expectations clear? Are you sure? (So often we *think* they are, but they're ambiguous at best.) Are your team's priorities and deadlines clear? Do they need more confidence, skill or motivation? Are they up to the job? Dig deep and see what you learn. Ask yourself what you would do first if you anticipated success for this team.

Example 2: Your boss is unsupportive. What can *you* choose to influence and change to get a different outcome?

Write down how *you* can help *your boss* be a better leader (counterintuitive, I know, but stick with it, and you'll see results). Ask them what they need more or less of from you. Tell them precisely what support you need and why. 'I'd like more time with you' is too vague. Instead suggest something concrete and give specific reasons for it: 'I'd like to set up a weekly twenty-minute check-in during this project so we stay on track.' Anticipate success before you go into your next discussion and plan accordingly.

A client of mine, Lynne, told me that her newish boss was unsupportive. Her boss thought 'support' meant copying Lynne into every email to keep her in the loop. Lynne wanted more opportunities to talk about a possible promotion, but she didn't say it, so her boss did not know what to do with her. Mind reading is not a skill many people possess. Lynne expected her boss to know what she wanted without her communicating it.

While we always have a choice, it's important to keep in mind that we can't influence everything. If you *can't* influence or change something, let it go. If you *can* influence or change something but are unsure where to start, get support and guidance from someone who can help you. This will save you hours of rumination and overthinking.

Belief 4: I make a decision and make it work for me

Have you ever caught yourself going around in a loop, asking, 'Should I do this or that?', weighing up pros and cons and what-ifs, but still not deciding? None of us has the gift of hindsight for the decisions we're making today. My rule of thumb when procrastinating over a decision is to do your due diligence, listen to your intuition and be mindful of any potential biases – but put a time limit on it. Make a decision and make it work for you. The longer you sit on the fence, the more painful your choice will be. (You'll find my decision-making checklist in the resources available at www.effortlessleaders. com/lynn-scott-leader-unlocked.)

🔍 CASE STUDY 1: Sophie

Whenever I spoke to Sophie, a managing director, she told me what her CFO was or wasn't doing and how he undermined her. She kept asking me, 'Should I fire him? Should I ignore him? Should I find a way to work with him?'

She struggled to decide one way or the other, and this lack of decisiveness led her to obsess over what he was or wasn't doing during her every waking hour. When she finally did what she knew she should have done all along and fired him her business began thriving under her stronger focus and leadership.

Belief 5: I have simple, consistent habits that energise me

As James Clear writes in his book *Atomic Habits*, 'Every action you take is a vote for the type of person you wish to become.'[2] Success comes when we break our big goals into small, actionable daily tasks. The easier the task, the easier it is to make into a habit. I wanted to be an author (hey, I am an author), so my starting task was to write every day for ten minutes. When that felt like a breeze, the task became writing for thirty minutes a day. It's a full day at a time in the final draft stages.

---

2   Clear, J, *Atomic Habits: An easy and proven way to build good habits and break bad ones* (Cornerstone Press, 2018)

Our brains are wired to favour routine and conserve energy. This means some of your current autopilot habits and beliefs may prevent you from becoming who you want to become and achieving what you want to achieve. I wasted some of my best hours going down rabbit holes. When I stopped checking my emails, news feed and socials first thing in the morning and instead spent five minutes anticipating success for the day ahead, I became more productive and focused.

You, too, have habits that don't align with the person you want to become. Change one thing at a time and make it so easy that you can't fail to do it. You can choose a goal or habit and stick to it. Imagine taking five minutes at the beginning of your workday, for example, to ground yourself and anticipate success rather than diving straight into emails. Tell yourself, 'I am someone who plans and prioritises my day'. Your brain will find myriad ways to help you be that person. It's powerful and energising.

📑 CASE STUDY 2: Alli

Alli was twitchy about taking time out to think and reflect. She began with an hour a week. (I ask all my clients to start here.) These days, she goes off-grid twice a month, blocking out what she calls 'focus days'. Being away from her desk helps, because her desk means emails, which mean distraction.

Alli can proudly say, 'I am someone who knows the value of deep, focused work, and my results prove it.' Her results do indeed prove it. She has strengthened her stakeholder relationships and lobbied for her department and is influencing change at the highest level.

Belief 6: I have a positive attitude toward myself

Whatever you believe about yourself tends to become a self-fulfilling prophecy. Lose the old, worn-out labels and instead choose a label you love and can wear with pride. What's the Chanel version of you like?

Compare the beliefs in the table below. Note the differences in belief between the left and right columns. How might the beliefs expressed affect your actions, choices and behaviour?

Negative vs. positive beliefs

Negative beliefs about myself	Positive beliefs about myself
I'm a people pleaser.	I'm kind *and* I have clear boundaries.
I'm not a confident presenter.	I'm building my confidence by presenting every day.
I'm too much in the detail.	I'm learning to see the bigger picture.
I've got imposter syndrome.	I'm growing into my role every day.

Labels

Putting the six core beliefs to work

Let's look at how you can use these six core beliefs to make changes right now:

- Anticipate success as you consider the first change you want to make.

- Write down everything that springs to mind when you consider this change.

- Notice your choices: saying no instead of yes, being available or unavailable, setting boundaries or not, speaking up or staying quiet. Be aware of any default habits that might get in your way, for example, never speaking up during project meetings even though you have lots of ideas.

- Choose one small thing you can change this week – or right now.

- This change should energise and excite you when you think about it. If you need help with execution, ask a trusted ally who will have your back.

- Do the thing.

Once you discard your old unhelpful ways of being and doing, you'll find new ways of defining yourself.

Being open to the possibility that we can change something (even if we don't know *how* yet) is crucial to our success. So is our willingness to experiment. We don't have to do it all at once; remember we've established a six-month timeline. In the next chapter, we'll discuss ways of using that time more wisely. First, here are your key takeaways from this chapter.

Key takeaways

- Our beliefs shape everything, but generic, fluffy 'think positive' doesn't change much.

- Beliefs tend to become self-fulfilling prophecies. Six non-negotiable beliefs are fundamental to your leadership success.

- Anticipating success as you begin a task primes your brain to find ways to succeed.

- Start working on your goal or task even if the circumstances aren't perfect.

- Don't delay making difficult decisions. Rather than ruminating, make a choice and make it work for you.

- Start small with a new habit and build on it – five minutes this week, ten minutes next week. Consistency is key.

- Recognise any negative thought patterns. Recognising them is the first step to changing them.

2
The 'Busyness Is Laziness' Paradox

In Chapter 1, we learned some non-negotiable beliefs that will help you succeed. In this chapter, we will get rid of another belief: *I don't have time*. This belief creates a self-fulfilling prophecy of – you've guessed it – not enough time. We're not buying into that belief anymore.

If your organisation feels chaotic and overwhelming, you can either collude with the chaos and join the 'I'm so busy' club, or you can do something different. Mental overload, decision fatigue, information saturation and overwhelm are among the biggest barriers to strong leadership focus, presence, impact and gravitas and the biggest causes of stress, exhaustion and burnout. If everything is a priority, nothing is a priority. Go back to first principles and clarify your top three to five priorities.

You'll reduce your heavy load before anything else, starting with one simple activity that will make the most significant difference to your focus, effectiveness and success: *making time for it*. Notice I say *make* time, establishing a proactive approach. *Hoping* some time will magically appear rarely works. In this chapter, I'll share several strategies and practical activities that will lighten your leadership load and help you slow things down so you are able to move forward intentionally.

Stop being lazy

'Me? Lazy? Are you kidding? I never stop,' you say. I argue, however, that always being 'on' can be a form of laziness. It's easier for your brain to stay on busy autopilot than step back, think, plan and clarify priorities. That's why there is so much headless-chicken behaviour in organisations whose direction, strategy and goals are unclear.

Make it a habit to give yourself down time so you can work more intentionally. When it comes to saving or finding time, there's one great question to ask yourself every so often: what am I doing that is stupid? Ask this question, and you'll get all sorts of answers and ideas of things to change. (Ask your team the same question and be prepared for some interesting observations!)

Be kind to your brain

Your prefrontal cortex is located behind your fore-head. You can think of it as your third eye of wisdom. It's the part of the brain involved in higher-order functions like decision-making, problem solving, planning, goal setting and regulating emotions. You know that adequate sleep, regular exercise and a healthy diet are important for your well-being. They're also essential for good brain function. If you're in daily back-to-back meetings with no breaks, your brain can become tired. When you're mentally fatigued:

- Your powers of influence are diminished

- You make mistakes

- You can't focus

- You ruminate and overthink

- You don't listen well

- You react without thinking

- You feel frantic and disorganised

- You lose confidence and impact

- You're not leaderlike

You can't think straight because your brain is over-loaded and trying to conserve energy.

If you struggle with having too much to do and not enough time, I hear you. For years, I wore my 'busy' label as a badge of honour. I thought, *Look at me. Aren't I indispensable, important, in demand?* Er, no. Reality check: you're too busy because you find it hard to say 'no' and are not prioritising or thinking strategically (because you don't think you know how). Let's move away from 'busy' and towards 'effective' and 'productive'. Put on your anticipate-success hat, and let's go.

The success hat

Rethink busyness

What gets rewarded gets done, and that can sometimes be bad news. If time spent at work is how we measure dedication rather than output and results, we will always create more 'busy' work.

Being visibly busy is 'good', whereas staring out of the window or going for a walk means 'you don't have enough to do'. It's 'better' to be seen at all those meetings than gain valuable insights by letting your mind wander free, eh?! Presenteeism is the enemy of productivity.

That's why having white space in your calendar feels counterintuitive when the work is piling up. Let's turn this thinking on its head.

I don't know about you, but I get my best ideas when I'm not trying too hard – in the garden, in the shower or walking the dog. The best leaders you know don't rush from pillar to post day after day, week after week, with no time to think. (Don't believe me? Ask them!)

What's the difference between the calm, considered, well-prepared leader who listens well and talks clearly and succinctly and the frantic, rushed leader who wings it, arrives late, is stuck in the weeds and disorganised? They may both be talented, clever and experienced, but which one exudes confidence? Which one inspires trust and helps you flourish? Which one is more effective and demonstrates confidence? Which one demonstrates, 'I've got this'? *I guarantee* that the first leader has deliberately created time in their calendar to think, reflect, prepare, connect and let their mind wander free. You can try this with Activity 2.

🔆 ACTIVITY 2: Create your space time

I ask clients to block at least one hour a week as white space – a blank space in the calendar – for time to think, or 'space time'. I also ask them to forever more block out twenty minutes a day, forty-five minutes twice a week, or ninety minutes once a week to do what I loosely call 'the strategic stuff' or 'the important stuff'. Some leaders like to take more time than this. Don't overthink it. Make a decision and remember that you can add more time later (but please don't subtract). Get comfortable with that and you can then add 'buffer zone' time – for those things that will inevitably come up in your working day.

Get your calendar and do this now.

Your space time is sacrosanct. Be uncontactable. The world will keep turning. If you're thinking, *No way*, remember what I told you in the last chapter: even if you commit just five minutes of space time daily to quiet reflection before turning your laptop on, you're starting as you mean to go on, and you can build on that habit. Tell yourself, *I am someone who knows the value of good thinking time.*

Yes, that's you. Nice label. Finding what I call a 'space place' conducive to good thinking will make it even better. You might also take your thoughts for a walk and see what great ideas and wisdom emerge.

Connect space and success

More space time equals more resourcefulness. When you feel better resourced, you feel more confident, in control and able to listen and make decisions. You're more present and your brain works at its best. Here's what some of the leaders I work with say about their space time:

Tim says, 'We have "boulder" space booked out in our calendars for our big goals.[3] Nobody can interrupt that space – company rule.'

We started 'Big Boulder Monday' in my most recent 'Lead with Confidence' programme. It is an excellent way to anticipate success as we start the week ahead.

Some years ago, **Juliette** said, 'If I have all that free time blocked out, what will my executive assistant think I'm doing?'

To which I replied, 'Why don't you enlighten her?'

Paul dedicates ninety minutes every Monday to work with his deputy on key projects that, much to his boss's frustration, have been on the back burner for months. Paul's boss is delighted that Paul has prioritised this and the work is being completed after many 'too busy' excuses.

---

3   Covey, S, 'The "big rocks" of life!', Apple Seeds, www.appleseeds. org/Big-Rocks_Covey.htm, accessed 23 September 2024

David dedicates Wednesday mornings to upskilling the marketing team – work he'd meant to delegate for ages. With new venture capital funding for his growing business, he must step away from details and focus on growth. The difference in his confidence, impact, motivation, headspace and focus is palpable. His team's confidence and skill are growing. Win-win.

Nicola, an NHS Clinical Director, 'reclaimed' two hours a week implementing the practices in this chapter. She managed to do this during the winter, the NHS's busiest and most challenging time of the year, when much of the work is unavoidably reactive. She'll find even more time in the spring, because she's made 'white space' a habit and is building on it.

Overcoming the cultural BS

Worried about what the 'busy people' might think? As Tim Ferris writes in his book *The Four-Hour Work Week*, 'Slow down and remember this: Most things make no difference. Being busy is a form of mental laziness.'[4] Hold your nerve and guard your space time, whatever the doubters say.

Once you experience the power of white space and space to help you do important things, you'll block out much more of it – before meetings, after meetings,

---

4   Ferris, T, *The Four-Hour Work Week: Escape 9-5, live anywhere, and join the new rich* (Vermilion, 2011)

instead of meetings. If you don't believe you can find time in your working week, you likely have a severe cognitive overload problem (but you already know that, don't you?). When you give yourself space time, you can see more clearly and the mist disappears. As the doubters see how much more leaderlike you are, they'll want what you're having.

Lighten the load

Once you've tried on those six foundational beliefs for size, anticipated success and created your space time, try Activities 3, 4, 5 and 6. These are practical activities intended to lighten your cognitive load. Doing just one of them regularly will significantly impact your time and energy.

☀ ACTIVITY 3: Close the open loops

Write down everything you have to do that's in your head but not on your calendar. Include work, family and everything else, however small, in no particular order. Use whole sentences that start with a verb. Verbs imply movement and direction, and the brain is naturally drawn to action words.

Your list might look like this:

- Phone the electrician for a quote
- Block out June holiday dates
- Order printer ink

'Seriously, Lynn?' you might be saying. 'Shouldn't I be prioritising *big, important things*?'

I'm glad you asked.

All those open loops and unfinished tasks take up lots of mental space, as if someone is sitting on your shoulder saying, 'You've not forgotten that, have you?' I have a big whiteboard in my office where I write all of these things down, and I address them once a week. Once they're written down, I no longer waste time remembering them.

Try it. You'll feel lighter, less cluttered and more in control.

ACTIVITY 4: Time blocking

A 2022 article in the *Harvard Business Review*[5] explains that digital workers spend just under four hours a week orienting themselves, toggling between emails, spreadsheets, apps, documents and websites.

Instead, try scheduling blocks of time for specific tasks. This is an excellent way to help your executive brain. It can help you focus and avoid a lot of toggling that is cognitively taxing and wastes time.

For me, this might mean taking a morning to write a month's worth of posts for my newsletter or my

---

5   Murty, RN, Dadlani, S and Das, RB, 'How much time and energy do we waste toggling between applications?', *Harvard Business Review* (29 August 2022), https://hbr.org/2022/08/how-much-time-and-energy-do-we-waste-toggling-between-applications, accessed 16 August 2024

Facebook group (you'll find details on how to sign up for these at the end of this book). For you, it might mean dedicating your final hour of the work day to responding to emails. Block out time on your calendar for tasks you otherwise struggle to keep up with and see how much mental energy you set free.

🔆 ACTIVITY 5: Inbox zen

These are my ten favourite inbox timesavers. Give them a try. You'll be surprised how big a difference they make.

1. Take yourself off a circulation list or five – lists that add no value to your work or master lists you don't need to be on.

2. Unsubscribe from newsletters and promotional emails. Several apps make this a breeze. Saves you money, too.

3. Ask your team to email you *only* if they need your input. You don't need to be copied into every long email trail. If this suggestion makes you twitchy, ask yourself why that is. Figure out the answer and decide what to do about it.

4. Picture this: someone sends you an email that goes on forever. You're not clear what they want, so you go back to them and the process repeats. Or maybe someone copies everyone in on passive-aggressive emails 'for information' (yeah, right). People on the circulation list then dive in to defend, justify, attack

and cover their collective backside. The lesson? Much of the time, all this can be avoided with a quick conversation.

5. Turn off all those pinging email notifications. Reading a notification while you're trying to do something else reduces your cognitive capacity and impact.

6. Set an out-of-office message for when you're focusing on something important, for example, 'I'm using this afternoon to focus on project X – I will be back online tomorrow morning.' I'd love you to say, 'I'm using this time to look out of the window and get my best ideas,' but that might be a bridge too far. For now.

7. Use clear subject headings in emails so the recipient knows what to do. Is your email for information only (FYI) or for action (FYA). Are you making a request, or do you need a decision? 'Sign-off needed by Friday' is clearer, for instance, than 'urgent response required', because your definition of 'urgent' might not be someone else's. 'Help needed' is likewise vague; just come out and ask for what you need.

8. Get to the ******* point. Readers want to know what to do immediately when they open your email. 'Bottom line up front' is a good rule of thumb.

9. If you have an assistant, get them working on your behalf on all things email. Many leaders do not use their assistants as well as they could.

10. Try to reduce the word count of your email by half. In days gone by, when messages were passed by telegram, every single letter used cost money. As a result, telegrams were short and to the point.[6] These days, of course, there are plenty of AI tools help you write more succinctly

☀ ACTIVITY 6: Team check-in

At the same time each day or each week, do a quick verbal check-in with your team (individually or collectively). This check-in should be time-bound and ask one key question: 'What do you need from me to make progress on your big goals today (or this week)?'

This habit saves a tremendous amount of email traffic and avoids those 'Have you got a minute?' interruptions that can derail you. A *note of caution, however:* your role is to coach, guide and help employees find solutions, not do their work for them.

This activity works well for several of my leadership clients. Tweak it to make your version. Use my WATERS framework in Chapter 15 to help you.

---

6 You'll find more great email tips here: Sehgal, S, 'How to write email with military precision', *Harvard Business Review* (22 November 2016), https://hbr.org/2016/11/how-to-write-email-with-military-precision, accessed 16 August 2024

Embrace the (slower) pace

While your work rate is undoubtedly phenomenal, there are times when slowing down can make you even more phenomenal. When you have lots to do, the temptation is to keep pushing through. That's only sustainable in the short term. Instead, make Activities 7 and 8 part of your success strategy and see how much wiser you become when you slow down.

> ### ☀ ACTIVITY 7: What are you feeling?
>
> Next time you catch yourself going down a rabbit hole or mindlessly scrolling, stop and ask yourself what you're feeling. What would you like to feel instead? Find a way to generate that feeling (see more on how to make your feelings work for you in Chapter 9).
>
> You may need to change your physiology by stretching or getting up and moving to more easily generate the new feeling. Fifteen minutes is all you need. This is a simple but powerful trick that works like a dream.

> ### ☀ ACTIVITY 8: The power of the pause
>
> Buy (or imagine having) a pause button.
>
> Pausing is your friend. It gives you breathing space (literally and metaphorically). It helps you listen better,

make better choices and buy yourself time. Rather than reacting and regretting, when you pause, you make more intentional decisions and communicate with more consideration. Rather than talking to fill space, you allow others to speak. Rather than getting caught in 'Have you got a minute?' conversations, you can say, 'I'm not free right now, but come back at 3pm.' A five-to-seven-second pause is all you need. It's the simplest and most effective time-saver I know.

PAUSE

5-7 SECONDS

The pause button

📑 CASE STUDY 3: Amy

Amy felt overwhelmed as a tight deadline for a big product launch approached. Her normal overwhelm strategy was to avoid thinking about the deadline and respond to mindless emails. This is the 'flight' response in action, running away from the looming deadline 'threat' – in other words, procrastination.

When I asked her how she wanted to feel, she said, 'Calm and in control.' I asked how she could generate that feeling of calm and control. Going for a walk typically calmed her down, but this time it didn't. 'My head is too busy,' she said.

Instead, she poured everything from her head onto a big sheet of paper. Her next step was to organise each item into prioritised actions. Once she did that, she felt calmer. She was now ready to walk in the park, where she could let her mind wander and get creative.

There is always a way to generate a feeling you want to feel.

In this chapter, we learned that establishing a space time habit helps our prefrontal cortex to be less overwhelmed, allowing us to think more clearly. We can take care of the more important and strategic things on our to-do list when we intentionally make time for them. We might even find that other people notice the change and follow suit. In the next chapter, we'll look at how you can master meetings. And save yourself even more time. But first, your key takeaways.

Key takeaways

- Create 'space' time to work through the activities in this book. Make it a priority rather than just trying to 'fit it in'. Create space to do your best thinking and make it a non-negotiable habit. Five minutes a day is better than no minutes a day.

- Introduce some tactical and practical ways to manage your time and inbox, replacing old habits with better ones.

- Avoid the distraction rabbit hole by recognising how you want to feel and prioritising actions that will get you there.

- Buy yourself time, recognise moments of choice and communicate more clearly using your pause button.

3
Meetings Mastery

How many meetings do you attend each week and say afterwards, 'Well, that was a waste of time?' No wonder meetings are often referred to as 'collective procrastination'. In this chapter, we'll learn how to change your meetings from dull to dynamic starting with what we can influence: the meetings we lead. Next, we'll zone in on the time-wasting meetings we're invited to.

Here's a question to get you thinking: why are my meetings so successful? If you're scratching your head and saying, 'But they're not,' I want you to anticipate success for your next meeting and see what ideas emerge.

Here's a truth you might not want to hear: if you're doing the dreaded 'go round the room and tell me what you're working on' routine, I guarantee that even if *you* find it helpful, everyone else is dying of boredom.

Meetings – firm foundations

I recently worked with a group of lawyers who wanted to reduce their one-hour team meetings to forty-five minutes but were worried that they wouldn't have enough time to get everything done. Once they had an outcome-focused agenda (see Activity 11), however, they found limiting meeting length was simple. Here's the lesson: if you *decide* you will have enough time and anticipate success, you'll make it happen. If it doesn't work, work out why and change it.

Time-out between meetings is not a 'nice to have', it's essential. Research from Microsoft Human Factors Lab[7] shows that when virtual meeting participants are deprived of breaks, their stress levels spike. The antidote to this is short breaks between meetings (obviously). This time is to clear your head – a few stretches, a walk, a comfort break, a glass of water. A short meditation (the research participants in the Microsoft study used a meditation app), some intentional breathing exercises, listening to some music. 'I'll just send this email before the next meeting' is a distraction, not a break. You'll feel different and be more leaderlike when you're not cramming 'just one

---

7   Microsoft Human Factors Lab, 'Research proves your brain needs breaks', Microsoft (20 April 2021), www.microsoft.com/en-us/worklab/work-trend-index/brain-research, accessed 16 August 2024

more thing' in. Make sure that everyone gets at least a ten-minute break between one meeting and the next; it's simple kindness for the brain.

How much? There are several meeting cost calculators and plugins available that give you an idea of how much time (and therefore, money) you spend on meetings. Do the math, as the Americans say. Is that time and money well spent?

Activities 9 through to 11 will help you lay the foundations for great meetings.

☼ ACTIVITY 9: Using Parkinson's law of meetings

Parkinson's Law states that our workload expands to fit the time we allocate for it. If we allocate one hour for a meeting, we will fill one hour. Simply reducing one-hour meetings to forty-five or fifty minutes can be all it takes to reduce the boredom and time wasted in overlong meetings. You can also try reducing thirty-minute meetings to twenty minutes.

☼ ACTIVITY 10: Design your rules of engagement

Tell your team that you want to improve meetings and save time. No one will argue with that. Ask them (so they own it) to create some rules of engagement for more effective, purposeful, engaging or inclusive meetings. These rules can be both tactical and behavioural.

Once you've established guidelines, it's up to everyone to actively make them work (not just you to police them). A ground rule about listening to each other is pointless if no one holds themselves and each other accountable.

Don't just go with the usual 'listen well' and 'don't interrupt' rules, although they are good ones to include. Think about how you might deal with groupthink or conflict or the elephant in the room. Or the people who don't know when to shut up. Be bold.

For example, I have just started working with a team that is caring and supportive of each other. However, it emerged in their Team 360 that they are not addressing some tensions and perceived unfairness (this can be the downside of an overly supportive team: challenging conversations are avoided). When I next see them, I will ask them how they want to handle unfairness or tension with care so they can include it in their rules of engagement.

💡 ACTIVITY 11: Write an outcome-focused agenda

An outcome-focused agenda circulated in advance tells people what they're in the meeting for. Think of your agenda as a set of questions to be answered or decisions to be made. Be clear about the purpose of each item; if an item is on the agenda for an update or informational purposes, say so. It's even better to allocate a specific time to each agenda item. Consider also how many agenda items you can realistically get through to get the best decisions or outcomes.

The following table provides two simple examples of an agenda. In the first, attendees have no clue why they're there. In the second, attendees are crystal-clear.

'Why am I here?' agendas vs. outcome-focused agendas

The 'why am I here?' agenda	The outcome-focused agenda
Customer complaints	Action: Agree on specific actions to reduce customer complaints by 15% in Q3 – 20 minutes
Staff turnover	Update: Reduce call centre turnover. HR will present its key strategies. Bring your questions – 25 minutes
Steve's new project	Information: Project scope overview, timeline, deliverables and budget. Steve – 15 minutes
Conference	Ideas for our 2026 Conference. Question: How can we make this our best conference yet? Open discussion.

Let people know what preparation you want them to do in advance. I work with one team that gets people together an hour before the meeting officially starts to do the prereading. No more 'Sorry, I was too busy to prepare' excuses there.

Saying no to pointless meetings

You know how to run better meetings now, so let's turn to avoiding meetings that do not work for you. 'Lynn, it's hard to say no,' you say. Not true. It's only hard if you *think* it's hard and if your priorities are unclear. Every time you say 'yes' to a meeting, you are, in effect, saying 'no' to something else – possibly something more critical. Any meeting that doesn't contribute to your organisational or personal goals can be shelved. Activities 12 and 13 can help you weed out the meetings that add no value.

☀️ ACTIVITY 12: Look back to look forward

Look back over the meetings you attended over the last three months and ask yourself:

- Which ones saved time, made decisions and got the right things done?

- Which ones did you attend with another team member? Does the meeting really need two of you?

- Which meetings are wishy-washy talking shops? (Definitely stop going to those.)

- If you didn't go to the meeting, would it matter?

- If you must attend the meeting, how can you make it better?

Decide which meetings you will stop attending or delegate to someone else. Activity 13 will help with this.

⚡ ACTIVITY 13: Say no to meetings without offending

When declining a meeting, it's best to be straightforward, give clear reasons and suggest an alternative, if appropriate. For example:

- I'm on a deadline with Project X, so I'll attend the first/last fifteen minutes.

- I won't be attending. I do have ten minutes before/after to answer any questions.

- I will take myself off this project group for three months while focusing on Project X.

- Sam will be attending this one from now on. She's closer to the detail.

- I've made it a rule not to attend meetings without an agenda. This helps me prioritise. Please send one over and let me know why you need me there.

- This meeting does not align with my current priorities, so I must decline. I'll let you know if things change.

Declining meeting invitations in this way should avoid offending others. If someone chooses to take offence, that's on them, not you.

Top tips for meetings

Once you're in the meeting room, the following four tips will help you stay on-schedule, ensure equal contribution, build relationships and get things done.

Start and end on time

In my own meetings, I allow no more than two minutes for people to arrive and reserve five to ten minutes at the end for everyone to briefly summarise their actions and commitments. Your own timing may vary, but you should tell people explicitly that this will happen and include it in your rules of engagement. When people know your meetings always start late, they'll keep arriving late – a vicious circle. And you're annoying as hell if your meetings always overrun. Surprise people by finishing five minutes early from now on.

Check in

The check-in is one way to build connection and appreciation as a team. Many teams I work with do this in a slightly longer monthly or quarterly team meeting. Ploughing through an agenda has its place, but 'time to breathe' conversations build relationships and collaboration. Genuine appreciation increases oxytocin, the hormone and neurotransmitter responsible for positive emotions such as trust and happiness, in the room. The questions can be quick-fire or more reflective. One team I work with has a monthly 'share what's on your mind' meeting that flows freely but is still outcome-focused. One minute per person is allowed to get something off their chest before moving on. The team then decides what they want to talk more about and what outcomes they'd like as a result. Another has a monthly 'celebrate success' check-in so they remember what they've achieved and recognise the challenges they've overcome. Cake and other treats are always provided.

Open the car park

Sometimes people go off on a tangent in meetings, potentially derailing the agenda. The quick and easy solution to this problem is to have a metaphorical 'car park' where any ideas that need to be dealt with are 'parked' and dealt with later by the individuals concerned. You might use the whiteboard method we discussed in Chapter 2 for this purpose. Include the car park in your rules of engagement.

Control conversation dynamics

'How do I get the talkers to shut up and the quiet ones to speak up?' you might be asking. Worrying about seeming rude or picking on people can get in the way here, but these eight tips will help you:

1. Ask your team to consider equality of contribution when they write the rules of engagement (see Activity 10).

2. Keep in mind that some people like to think out loud even when their ideas are not fully formed. This might be good for them, but it is not so good for us. Make a rule that everybody shares their

ideas in one minute or in three to four succinct bullet points.

3. Use the outcome-focused agenda (Activity 11) to help those who prefer to process information internally before speaking up. They'll be more prepared if they're asked a question later. Frame questions as an invitation to contribute rather than putting someone on the spot, for example, 'Sam, we've not heard from you yet, and I know you've done some interesting work on this – is there anything you'd like to say?' *Better still*: give the quieter or more reflective team members a heads up when you'd like their contribution, so they can think and prepare in advance.

4. In larger meetings, ask people to pair up, giving them specific questions to discuss. One of each pair then shares their ideas with the group. This is a surefire way to ensure everyone contributes and works with virtual breakout rooms, too.

5. Use the chat function in virtual meetings. You can pose specific questions like 'What's the best idea you've heard so far?' You can then say, 'Faye, you've chosen Idea A. Can you tell us more?'

6. If you agree with someone else's words, simply say 'agree'.

7. If you disagree, you can say, 'That's interesting. I have a different perspective but would like to hear more about yours.' This is a nonjudgemental

response that opens a dialogue rather than closing it down.

8. Be explicit about what engagement looks like, especially in virtual meetings. Should people stay on mute or not? Should cameras be on or not? Should people use the 'raise hand' function if they have something to say?

In this chapter, we discussed how to make meetings work for us and our team. We've learned ways of planning effective, dynamic meetings that are outcome-orientated. We've also learned some strategies for declining invitations to meetings that don't align with our priorities. You can now say, 'I am someone who uses my precious time well and values other people's time too.'

When you've freed up some time and space, you're ready for what comes next.

But first, your key takeaways.

Key takeaways

- Improve the meetings you organise and lead. Be transparent about the changes you're making and why.

- Rules of engagement make your meeting behaviours explicit. Ask your team to design these and own them – review them from time to time and tweak as needed.

- The outcome-focused agenda gives your meeting a clear purpose and structure.

- Say no to those meetings that don't contribute to your most important goals by clearly stating why you will not attend and providing an alternative where appropriate.

- Use the conversational dynamics tips I share to weed out the wafflers and encourage others to speak.

4

Visualise The Leader
You Want To Become

W hen we know where we're going, we set out
intentionally and with purpose, following our
north star. I designed this book and the activities in
it in part to free up your brain and calendar first so
you can start the more profound and fundamentally
life-changing work of connecting with the person and
leader you want to become – Future You.

I first came across the idea of Future You in an article
in *Harvard Business Review*, and started to create the
'future' version of me with the support of my own
coach.[8] This has been so fundamentally liberating and
life-changing that I've made it the golden thread that

---

8   Hardy, B, 'Take ownership of your future self', *Harvard Business
     Review* (August 28, 2020), https://hbr.org/2020/08/take-ownership-
     of-your-future-self, accessed 9 October 2024

runs through all of my coaching programmes. And I want to share it here with you, too.

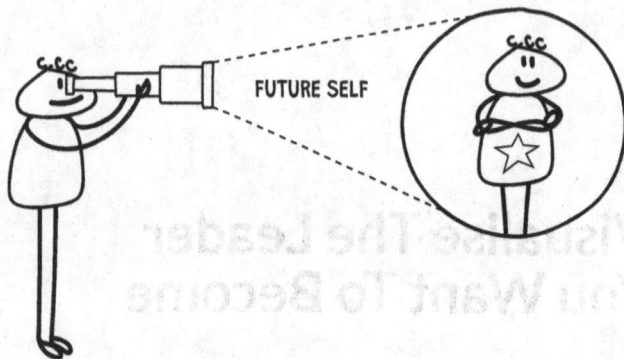

FUTURE SELF

Meet Future You

So, the big question now is, who do *you* want to become? The future version of you will be the leader *you* decide to become when you make decisions intentionally rather than pounding away non-stop on the organisational treadmill. To discover Future You, you will let go of the baggage and old scripts weighing you down or holding you back. You will recognise the beliefs and thoughts that block your path to success and find better ones that propel you forward, replacing old 'autopilot' habits with better habits. You will use your strengths and superpowers more often. The hardest part of this process for many of us is *believing* that we can change all of this. If you're saying 'It's just the way I am' you're lying to yourself. It's the way you're choosing to be. If you say 'I've tried to change before, and it's not worked' there will be a piece of the jigsaw you weren't aware of. The great news is that we all have the ability to rewire those old neural pathways and to remove the unhelpful labels we've given ourselves.

When you consistently practise new behaviours, habits or thoughts and try on new labels for size, you strengthen the neural circuits that support them. Decide today, for example, that you want to be a calm, focused unruffled leader rather than a leader who is frazzled and permanently stuck in the weeds and then start to make it happen one tiny step at a time. (This book will give you everything you need to do that.)

Because repetition is fundamental to habit formation, I'll repeat the question I asked in the introduction several times throughout the book: Imagine you and I meet for a drink six months from now. You say, 'I want to tell you about all the great things that have happened since I read your book.' What are you telling me? Activities 14 and 15 will help you to clarify your answer.

:🔆: **ACTIVITY 14: Visualise a different life**

Fast forward to six months from now. Put a big star in your calendar on that date. Imagine your best friend or someone you admire asking, 'Why are you so much more successful (confident, happy, fulfilled, relaxed, calm, motivated, at ease etc.) than you were six months ago? What changed?'

What do you tell them? You might say, for example: 'I'm so much happier than I was six months ago

---

because I stopped working out of hours and had more weekends away.' You might also say, 'I'm so much more confident than I was six months ago because I said yes to more opportunities and set clearer boundaries.'

Once you're 'there' in your mind, ask yourself how this future feels, looks and sounds. As you answer these questions, notice any negative thoughts you may have, such as, 'That'll never happen'. Notice, accept and think about how you might exchange them for some anticipate-success thoughts (we will dig much deeper into this in Chapter 7). Make some notes. You're previewing what's to come, and we'll revisit the question later in this chapter, where you'll create and align with Future You in glorious, surround-sound Technicolour, Hollywood Blockbuster-style.

How does this Future You stuff work?

Research shows that visualisation improves performance – athletic performance, academic performance, even surgical skills. You perform better in the real world when you rehearse your desired outcomes. You see yourself succeeding, as capable and confident. You start to shift your identity and how you see and define yourself. That helps you keep going, feel motivated and make progress. It's like putting a photo on your fridge to remind you of the healthier person you'll be when you eat more vegetables and less cheesecake.

Repetition is the key to success, and repetitive visualisation can strengthen neural pathways related to specific skills or behaviours. You visualise yourself doing or saying something so you can start to do or say it for *real* today. Over time, your visualisation creates new neural pathways in your brain based on what you experience in the 'movie' you play in your mind. Doing this repeatedly reinforces those neural pathways, increasing your competence and confidence. Future You's way of approaching things becomes your new normal. (If you find you struggle with visualisation, I include other ways of bringing Future You to life later in this chapter.)

Before we continue, *let me be clear*: imagining, creating and growing Future You does not mean you are not good enough right now. You are not broken. Think of Future You instead as the version of you that has reached your highest potential, lives your best life (which is not about being perfect) and knows precisely what that means for you. Choose *your* version, not somebody else's. Think of visualisation as planting a mental Future You seed that you will nurture daily. Activity 15 will help you with this.

🔆 ACTIVITY 15: Fast forward rehearsal

Armed with the tips I shared in Chapter 3, anticipate success in your next team meeting. Imagine yourself in that meeting *right now*: you're nailing it. What do you notice? What do you feel?

Write it down or say it in the *present tense* because you imagine yourself in that meeting now. Don't answer the question hypothetically.

> **Example:** *I arrive on time, fully prepared, with my head held high, and everyone else arrives promptly. We've got a clear agenda and purpose. I ask incisive questions and receive well-thought-out responses. We make key decisions and agree upon actions. We're buzzing.*
>
> *I feel a sense of pride in my team, confident in my ability to motivate, inspire and keep everyone on track. Everyone's excited about where we're going, why and what we can achieve.*
>
> Once you've imagined it, you've seen it, so you know exactly what to do now to make the next meeting a success. This is how you prime your brain for success daily.

Slow down and enjoy the view

If you've completed the activities in this book so far (remember that doing them consistently over time will help you progress) you can probably see some light at the end of the tunnel. You have more space in your calendar and your meetings are shorter and more effective. You anticipate success daily and focus on what you can influence and change. You make decisions based on who you want to become, and these energise and excite you. You're less distracted and your pause button opens a new world of choice. As a result, you're more resourceful, confident and leaderlike and have found new ways to define yourself while shredding some old labels.

But what if that's not happening? Maybe instead of giving time and space to Future You, you've put it off until you're less busy, the kids are older, your partner retires or you've paid off the mortgage. Perhaps you're so used to putting your needs last that you've not allowed yourself to explore this question in depth. Sometimes there are valid reasons to hold fire. Often, though, it's fear or self-doubt that keeps us stuck in avoidance or procrastination. Let's be honest, 'I need to think about it' often means 'I don't want to think about it at all – it's too hard'. Maybe you like the ideas and activities in this book, but this deeper exploration of yourself and the idea of a Future You brings up some things you're not quite sure what to do with. It's certainly not what you've done in leadership programmes before. (Which is why not much has changed despite best intentions.)

Wherever you are right now is OK. If you've not changed anything yet, be curious rather than judgemental about why that is. Ask, 'What's stopping me?' or, 'What am I resisting?' Listen to your answers, then dig deeper. Ask yourself, 'If I put on my anticipate-success hat right now, would my answer change?'

No regrets

One of the books that has touched me profoundly is Bronnie Ware's *Top Five Regrets of the Dying*, written in 2012.[9] Ware, a palliative care nurse, worked with people who had gone home to die, remaining with them for the last three to twelve weeks of their lives. When she asked her patients if they had any regrets or what they would do differently, some common themes came up. According to Ware, these were the top five regrets of the dying:

- I wish I'd had the courage to live a life true to myself, not the life others expected of me.

- I wish I hadn't worked so hard.

- I wish I'd had the courage to express my feelings.

- I wish I had stayed in touch with my friends.

- I wish I had let myself be happier.

Every one of these things is within our sphere of influence. The more we wait for the 'perfect' time, the more moments and opportunities to be that courageous, joyful, confident, content future version of ourselves we lose right now.

Rather than focusing on what we don't want, it's better to use our energy to focus on what we do want. When we think about what we don't want, our brains automatically create an image of it. For example, if I tell you, 'Don't think of a green banana', what pops immediately into your head?

9   Ware, B, *The Top Five Regrets of the Dying: A life transformed by the dearly departed* (Hay House UK Ltd, 2012)

Exactly.

Feel the different energy in each of the following statements: 'I won't feel nervous in the meeting' can mean you focus on your nervousness, whereas 'I prepare myself and ask my questions in the meeting' means you focus on preparation and questions (rather than that nervousness). Or, 'I'm not at everyone's beck and call', vs. 'I have clear expectations, and everyone knows my boundaries'. Which statements inspire confidence and motivation? The difference may seem subtle – but it isn't. Try your own experiments with this and see what you notice.

Activity 16 expands on the visualisation you did in Activity 14. Case Study 4 should also provide you with some inspiration as you create your image of Future You.

☀ ACTIVITY 16: Future You: the blockbuster version

You asked yourself an important question in Activity 14 (the visualisation exercise): why am I so much more successful (etc.) six months from now? Next, we're going to visualise the Hollywood blockbuster version. If the method of visualisation from Activity 14 worked like a dream for you, stick with it for this activity. If it didn't, you can create that future version of yourself in several other ways. Feel free to experiment with any of these ten methods below to find what works best for you.

Tip: Write down or say out loud or visualise what you *want*, not what you *don't* want.

1. Brain dump or list: Write down everything you want to tell me in six months. Let your mind freewheel for now. You can make sense of it later, when you're ready.

2. Journaling: Write your Future You ideas down in the present tense as they come. No censoring. If you already write a daily gratitude journal, you might try writing an entry from the perspective of Future You, considering what Future You will be grateful for in six months.

3. Poem, story or song: You can write your own story, song or poem where you are the protagonist or hero. You can start with 'Once upon a time' or the opening line of a favourite song or write your own lyrics to the tune of a song you love – whatever gets your creativity going.

4. Letter from Future You: Write a letter to Future You to be delivered six months from now. Write in the present tense, using *I am* rather than *I will*. What would you like to read six months from now? You can set this up automatically (by email) at futureme.org.

5. Future You mantra: A mantra, or positive affirmation, is an empowering positive statement. The power of a mantra or affirmation lies in its daily repetition, which helps us form those new neural pathways.

Choose a mantra you can repeat to yourself when you need a confidence or Future You boost. Your mantra can be realistic and believable, bold and courageous – outrageous, even! Choose a mantra that is personal, specific and meaningful to you, rather than something performative (eg, 'I look good on Instagram.'). Again, use the present tense.

The following example mantras have had a significant positive impact on the success and confidence of both of their users, Sara and Monica. We will return to Monica in Chapter 6.

Monica: I'm cool, calm and collected.

Sara: We're shaking up the culture one conversation at a time.

6. Speaking out loud: Speaking aloud to someone with no agenda, who can listen well and ask questions that expand your Future You thinking, can have bigger benefits, as you get all your thoughts and ideas out of your head and can then start to make sense of them. You'll want to choose someone with no agenda who can listen well without interrupting and help you expand your Future You thinking. My husband talks to our cat, Bowser. It works for him.

7. Visualisation: Repeatedly creating mental images of your desired outcome can help turn those 'pipe dreams' into reality. It's always a present-tense exercise, but you can do it any time, any place, anywhere. You can also translate any visualisation experience into words or pictures later, if you choose, through drawing or the vision board (see below).

8. Going for a walk: If you want to shake things up, try taking the question out with you for a walk. Going to a different environment can get your creative juices flowing and can help get you unstuck.

A change in environment creates new stimuli for your brain and gives you a mental refresh that sparks new ideas. Different environments may trigger new associations and connections in your brain, encouraging creativity and innovation. Being in a calming or inspiring environment can reduce cortisol, the hormone associated with stress. We get our best ideas when we're not trying too hard.

9. Vision board: A vision board is a visual representation of your goals and desires. It's generally a collage of images, words, photos and symbols representing your aspirations. Choosing these images forces us to think deeply about what we want.

You can cut out or print pictures, phrases or words from magazines and newspapers that represent something you want and put them on a board. You can also try creating online vision boards on websites like Pinterest. Sometimes an image might speak to you, without your knowing why. Use it anyway; the meaning will become clearer somewhere down the line. Try working with a friend or coach to ask questions about your chosen images. The 'a-ha!' moments you get when you think deeply about these images can be breathtaking. Your subconscious mind is powerful. Tap into it.

10. Drawing: Drawing enables us to communicate emotions, experiences and abstract ideas that may be difficult to describe in words. The act of physically creating something engages multiple senses, making the experience impactful and memorable. Use images, shapes and colours to represent different ideas, allowing for a richer and more nuanced understanding of Future You. It's a compelling way to reveal hidden ideas in your subconscious. Don't worry if you're not 'artistic'; you don't have to be a budding Monet or Picasso. I recommend drawing the old-fashioned way, on a whiteboard, flipchart or notebook.

Drawing is inherently playful. My clients remember and still refer to their drawings from years ago. For example:

- **Marcus:** New managing director Marcus drew a big picture of the previous managing director with tiny stick figures looking up at her. He placed himself as a much smaller image at the top of the page. The drawing helped him see that he and his team needed to move on from the previous managing director's command-and-control-style leadership. So began Marcus's new approach to leadership.

- **Denise:** Denise drew a ball of tangled wool. This revealed that we needed to (metaphorically) find the end of the wool, so that she could start unravelling what was happening in her head. Once we finished, and some months later, Denise moved abroad and started a new career. She had to experience that unravelling before she could think clearly and make those big life decisions.

- **Finance team:** One of the team members drew the finance team as an old-fashioned record player with an old '78 going round and round. The team needed to become a higher tech and sleeker version of themselves. Years later, when they're stuck in 'same old', they still ask themselves, 'Is that old '78 playing again? What's the upgrade?'

📇 **CASE STUDY 4: Jane's Future You story**

Ultimately, if I want to be everything I know I can be, I must make better choices. Everything I am now reflects a choice I have made as an adult. Many challenges I am wrestling with result from being a 'yes' person. I've been prioritising work and others' happiness above myself and my loved ones. I know that doesn't make me a bad person, but it doesn't make me happy.

My future self is happy because I am in control and have balance in the following four key areas of my life:

- **Health:** I am pain-free. I can walk at least an hour a day with ease. I am in control of my diet. I have limitless energy. I wake up feeling ready to seize each day as it arrives. These things enrich my life by allowing me to spend more time outside in nature, exploring the beautiful coastline where we live with my family, friends and dogs.

- **Relationships:** I spend more time with my partner and children. I manage friends' expectations of what I can realistically give them. I have frequent quality time with my family. My relationship with my sister and her family is improved. I travel regularly. These things enrich my life by allowing me to spend more time with people who are important to me and do things that bring me joy.

- **Work:** I express myself clearly when under duress. I focus on delivering through people, helping us all grow and develop further. My influence within the organisation is growing. I feel fulfilled by my achievements. I work smarter, not harder. These things enrich my life by giving me control over how others impact me and how I support others in a balanced way.

- **Money:** I am in control of my finances. I have bought our next home and have sufficient funds to travel regularly. I am conscious that money cannot buy more time. I manage others' expectations about what I can provide. These things enrich my life because I spend money on things that I want, rather than what I am forced or feel obliged to.

I am a leader, mother, wife, daughter, friend, sister, colleague, coach and mentor. I am hugely empathetic, a good listener, reliable and helpful. Typically, I am pragmatic, a calming influence and solution- and action-orientated. I am extremely driven and fair, but I have a fierce sense of loyalty. I champion the underdog and others who are unheard. People turn to me in a crisis and trust me to go above and beyond to help. I thrive in the face of adversity. I bring calm to others, even when I am raging internally. My life experiences have blessed me with wisdom and an ability to tackle problems head-on.

As we've seen in this chapter, there are many ways to create Future You, and there are many ways to bring Future You to life. The following examples of Future Yous shared by my leadership clients will hopefully inspire you:

- **Ryan:** My team resolves everything operational and 'reactive'; anything escalated to me has followed the proper path. I feel positive due to our team's success and quality of service. All of our plans are well documented, our route map is clear and our projects are on-schedule.

- **Lynne:** Everyone on the Senior Leadership Team has signed up for the leadership approach and culture change I outlined last year. If they disagree with it, they've moved on. I feel lightness and energy as I see how the team is living our values, working together and blossoming. Anything feels possible now.

- **Monica:** I feel joy in my life and work. I'm less on edge, and my boys and partner get more of the 'fun Monica'. I spend more time with friends and family and feel present with them. I'm more measured and speak slowly and calmly. I have a great relationship with my new peers. Our purpose is clear and everyone has completely bought in to where we're going. I'm spreading my wings and the inadequacy I felt before is long gone. I know my worth. I'm cool, calm and collected. I've hit my £150K annual salary target and let 'manic Monica' go.

In this chapter, we discussed building a vision of the leader we want to become. We learned that if we want something to be different, we must start working toward it now. One tiny step is enough, and Future You will thank you for taking it. Chapter 5 contains a beautiful, brain-friendly way to keep Future You alive daily. We'll learn how to create a plan and get our brain to help us. First, your key takeaways.

Key takeaways

- There are lots of ways to bring Future You to life. Experiment with different methods until you find the ones that work best for you. There is no 'right' way to create or define Future You. There is only your way. And you don't have to do everything at once.

- Working toward Future You does not reduce the worth of Current You. You are not broken; you just have goals you're not yet reaching or aspirations you want to breathe life into. Future You *is* you reaching your full potential.

- Try stepping into your Future You shoes every day. As you imagine Future You, you create new neural pathways that override the old habits holding you back. The more you bring Future You to life, the stronger those neural pathways become.

- Consider which habits or aspects of your life might hold you back from working toward Future You. What do you need to do to make working toward Future You easier?

5
From Vision To Reality

You know what you want: the Future You movie is streaming, the words are spoken, the song is sung, the story is written and the vision board is colourful and bright. Now what? You may be tempted to stop now, thinking, *Nice, Lynn, but now back to the real world.*

You're not going to do that, though. Why would you? If the Future You you've created is not compelling, have another go. If it doesn't excite you, you may need to be bolder or more honest with yourself. Maybe you've put some imaginary roadblocks in the way. Maybe you're thinking, *I could never be that person in reality* or *There's no way this could happen.*

Is that actually true? Remember, Future You is not an imaginary person. It's you without all the metaphorical baggage. It's you after you've left the old stories and scripts behind you. It's you a few steps ahead of where you are now. Future You is still you. In this chapter, we will focus on one question that will help you make Future You the reality: *What would Future You want Current You to do right now?*

Find your sweet spot

I know I'm in the 'Future Me' zone when I'm inspired, excited and open to stretching my comfort zone with bolder, bigger and braver thoughts. That's my sweet spot. Do I wobble? Of course, but I know most of my wobbles are simply unhelpful mind chatter; they're not 'the truth'. The same is true for your wobbles.

Keeping Future You at the top of your mind every day makes it easy to become that person. Turning ideas into action requires that you turn your initial ideas into practical steps. You can do this by imagining a specific day in the life of Future You, from the moment you wake in the morning until you fall asleep at night. This exercise will take your visualisations to an even more granular level than you have so far. It's an important step that will take you within touching distance of the person you're becoming. Visualising this consistently will establish those strong new neural pathways that will make it easier to start taking small steps, one at a time, to turn your wishful thinking into grounded reality.

When self-doubt pops in, think of it as a sign that you're expanding, experiencing growth and trying to *become* more (but not *do* more). Self-doubt can be your friend, when you anticipate success. You get to choose what meaning you give to your self-doubt. You get to choose your thoughts about your self-doubt. Choose the thoughts that will take you *towards* Future You. Chapters 7 and 8 of this book will help you.

If you find this challenging, please know it's part of exploring and stretching your comfort zone. Ask yourself, *If this wasn't challenging, what would I do now?*

The reticular activating system

There is a super-simple way to keep Future You at the top of your mind daily: activating your reticular activating system (RAS). The RAS is the part of your brainstem that toggles between your conscious and subconscious minds. It helps you to stay awake, pay attention and process information. It's like a gate-keeper, taking in the information from your senses and filtering out everything *except* the information it thinks is important to your conscious mind.

When the RAS prioritises something, it signals the brain's cortex to wake up and pay attention. Any stimulus that says 'survival' or 'keep me safe' will get through the RAS unfiltered. It will also prioritise whatever you tell it is important. *That's the gold you need to remember.* The RAS notices what you pay attention to and sends it to the top of your conscious mind. Where your attention goes, energy flows. Suppose you've just bought a red car. Suddenly, you see red cars everywhere you look. Red cars have been around for a while, but your RAS hasn't deemed them important enough to pay attention to until now.

You can take advantage of this every day. For example, if you write meeting rules of engagement (Activity 10) and recognise, reward and reinforce the desired behaviours in every meeting, the RAS will make those rules second nature. If you have a screensaver or note that pops up first thing in the morning and says, 'Why was today a success?' you'll anticipate a successful day and plan accordingly. Use Activity 17 to help your RAS to focus and filter in the way that best serves your goals and aspirations.

ACTIVITY 17: Train your RAS

Put your vision board, drawing or mantra (Activity 16) somewhere you can see it regularly. If you do not have one, choose a couple of lines from one of your writing exercises to turn into a mantra.

The more you see this message, image or board, the more your RAS will help you focus on it. Looking at them occasionally will not be effective enough to make a difference. You must do it consistently to get results.

Remember Monica from Chapter 4? She put her mantra, *Cool, calm and collected*, on her vision board, where she could see it daily. Every day, before doing anything else, she used her pause button and asked herself questions like:

- How does a cool, calm and collected leader respond to this email?

- How does a cool, calm and collected leader ask for this pay rise?

- How does a cool, calm and collected leader run this team meeting?

Over a six-month period, repetition created new neural pathways that made that calm and measured behaviour – key to the senior role she's looking for – Monica's new default. Considering that her previous workplace nickname was 'Manic Monica', you can probably imagine how much of a shift this was for her.

Monica showed up differently when she anticipated success and channelled Future Monica. She learned, grew, stretched her comfort zone and made progress.

I had a Post-It note attached to my screen for a while that read, 'Published author'. I've now given myself an upgrade and changed it to 'Amazon bestselling author'. Will I make it? Maybe, maybe not, but that note helps me show up most days and write my heart out with you, my reader, in mind.

I guarantee you'll make progress once you've got your RAS on-side daily. You'll know where you're heading. You'll know what you want to tell me when we meet for that drink six months from now. There is no downside to this process. Enjoy the ride, whatever the final destination.

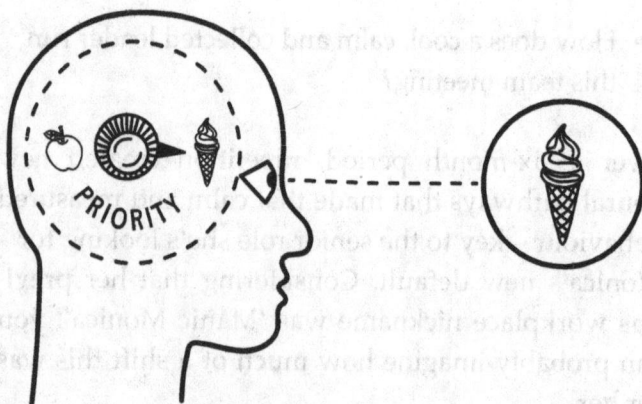

The reticular activating system

The clearer you are on where you're heading, the easier it will be to get there. In Activity 18, you will build on what you've created so far by gaining clarity on what happens in a day in the life of Future You. This will prime your brain for success.

💡 ACTIVITY 18: A day in the life of Future You

Picture this: you wake up tomorrow and a miracle has happened. Future You is here, right now, in glorious Technicolour. The day has come. You may want to choose a specific theme to focus on. For example, 'The Me that's been promoted' or 'The Me that's initiating successful culture change.' Or you may want to look at Future You more generally. These questions will help you see clearly what you're aiming for. Choose a few (or choose your own) and answer them in the present tense – remember, this makes it feel real and possible rather than hypothetical.

- What's the first thing you notice when you wake up?
- What do you do to prepare for the day ahead? What do you see, hear, feel or notice?
- What happens as you begin work for the day? What do you see, hear, feel or notice?
- What is the first thing you do to start your working day?
- How do you show up as a confident, competent leader?
- What happens during your first meeting or conversation of the day? What do you see, hear, feel or notice?
- What's going on with each of your team members? What do you see, hear, feel or notice?
- It's lunchtime. How is your day shaping up?
- What decisions are you making?
- What value are you adding to the world?

- What conversations are you having?
- In what ways do you feel valued and cared for?
- How does your working day end?
- What happens when you get home?
- How do you spend your family or private time?

Top tips for this exercise:

- Take your time. You will go back to this exercise again and again.

- Notice any resistance you might have to this exercise. Ask yourself *why* you are resisting. Be curious.

- If you're having difficulty, ask yourself, *If it were easy, what would I do now?* Then do it.

- Remember to do this activity in the present tense. You're feeling, seeing and doing it now. You're hearing those words now. You are quite literally creating your future.

In this chapter we learned that frequently imagining something – seeing it, being 'in the story' and feeling it – motivates us to find ways to make it happen. This is even better when our RAS is cheering us on. The cognitive priming effect we get when we spend some time getting our RAS involved will help us do the things that turn our hopes and ideas into reality. That's where we're going in Chapter 6: action! First, your key takeaways.

Key takeaways

- The RAS is the part of your brain that prioritises what to focus on. Get your RAS working for you every day by making Future You a daily focus.

- Choose an anticipate-success mantra and use it to help you centre Future You every day.

- Display your Future You mantra, vision board or drawing prominently. Pay attention to it every day. Where your attention goes, energy flows.

- Imagining a day in the life of Future You can give you clarity about what to do. It helps you see precisely how conversations, meetings, decisions and choices can and will be different.

6

The Path From Current You To Future You

You should be clear now on what Future You's life looks like – or part of it. If there's still some fuzziness, stick with it. Just keep allowing space and time to explore. Some things emerge slowly, others emerge quickly. All is well. In this chapter, you will learn to blaze a trail from Current You to Future You. Let's check my client Monica's progress from 'Manic Monica' to Future Monica as an example.

Before she came to me, Monica hadn't taken time out to contemplate what *could* be other than at the surface level. As we've discussed, slowing down to speed up is crucial when it comes to creating and aligning with Future You. This is why making space time in your calendar is a priority, not something to try to fit in among the noise. Monica realised that two thoughts had been keeping her from delegating her projects:

1. It's quicker to do it myself.

2. They won't do it as well as I can.

These thoughts may (or may not) be true, but they're not Future You thoughts. They are not cool, calm, collected leader thoughts. Once she recognised the thought that held her back, Monica chose a more empowering working thought: *With my guidance, my team will work well enough. I will start with one person and one task at a time. I can breathe.* She added *I can breathe* to her vision board.

Monica used six techniques to stay on track:

- She decided to make her progress one week at a time.

- Every day, she used her anticipate-success mantra, vision board and new *I can breathe* mantra to get her RAS working for her.

- She remembered to use her pause button to ask herself how a cool, calm, collected leader would handle each situation.

- She focused on thoughts that energised her and moved her forward, taking action from that place of energy.

- She made her garden her 'space place' and did her planning outside.

- She didn't give up when life threw a curveball (and it did). She took time to get back on

track and extended her six-month timeline to
nine months.

Monica made a series of conscious choices that ori-
entated her towards the 'Future Monica' leader she
wanted to become. She's on a path that will take her
from where she is now, to who she wants to become.
(Footnote: She got the promotion and pay rise she'd
imagined as Future Monica. Of course she did!)

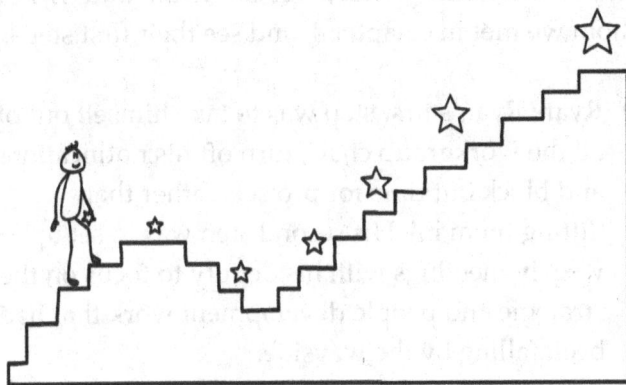

Walk on the way

The path from A to B

You are on a path from Current You (A) to Future You
(B). Like Monica, you decide how that path unfolds,
letting Future You guide you from A to B. You know
what Future You looks like and how Future You shows
up. You know the direction of travel. You get your
RAS working every day, focus on anticipate-success
thoughts and act based on those thoughts, one step

at a time. When setbacks happen, cut yourself some slack. If the path leads to dead ends, potholes or no-entry signs, re-focus and find your route back to Future You. All is well as long as you keep going.

When I say 'keep going', I don't mean keep going until you fall over and burn out. That is not the Future You we're aiming for. It's important to keep going in a brain-friendly way that optimises your brain and body for efficiency. Let's revisit Ryan and Lynne, whom we met in Chapter 4, and see their first steps:

- **Ryan:** Ryan's first step was to take himself out of all the workgroup chats, turn off his notifications and block out time for projects rather than 'fitting them in'. His second step was to set up weekly meetings with his deputy to focus on the strategic and people development work that had been falling by the wayside.

- **Lynne:** Lynne said, 'I changed my "I'll never get this done" and "there's so much to do" thinking. This meant my thoughts didn't become self-fulfilling prophecies.' After many years of deliberating, Lynne asked her assistant to take the leadership meeting minutes rather than do it herself. This gave her time to focus on the culture change and approach she wanted everyone to embrace.

As you chart the course from A to B, ask yourself what Future You would want Current You to do right now.

☀ ACTIVITY 19: Chart your path

Use these five questions to guide you in planning the path to Future You. I've shared Monica's responses to show you how this works in practice.

Questions	Monica's responses
1. On a scale of 1 to 10, how aligned are you with Future You?*	I'm a 7 – more than halfway there
2. Where would you like to be in six months? (Be realistically optimistic and anticipate success.)	I'd like to be a 9
3. What can you celebrate that's helped you reach your current level? (You can build on this as you progress.)	Clear direction and purpose that inspires My drive and ambition The way I care for my people Unwillingness to accept the status quo
4. List the changes that will get you to a 9. Your list should include actions and decisions you want to make, thoughts,** feelings, habits and behaviours you want to change and relationships you want to build. (You can expand on this list as you go.)	Believe in myself more Lose my perfectionism Be more present with my family Slow down and think before speaking Get to know my peers on a deeper level Speak more clearly and succinctly

(Continued)

Questions	Monica's responses
Tip: Help your brain. Write down what you want, not what you don't want.	Share my workload more
	Delegate key projects
	Apply for a promotion
	Build a wider profile
	Grow my senior stakeholder network
	Lose the 'Manic Monica' nickname
5. What will you choose*** to do this week that will take you closer to a 9? Ask yourself this question each week for six months and do the work required. Remember, small actions taken consistently are the key to success. Keep building those neural pathways.	Share and delegate my workload Week 1 – Decide which projects to delegate and to whom (sit in the garden to do this) Week 2 – Delegate Project 1 Week 3 – Delegate Project 2 Week 4 – Plan my 'profile build'

Notes:

* Question 1: How to score:

1 = I'm not off the starting block yet.
5 = I'm halfway there.
9 = I'm there.
10 = Perfection (which doesn't exist, so a nine is good enough).
Go with your 'gut feeling' for this.

** **Question 4:** 'Thoughts and feelings' work was a theme of my work with Monica. The item at the top of her list, 'Believe in myself more', was way too vague, so we broke it down into specific situations, devising different actions for each one. You almost *always* need to change your thoughts and beliefs about yourself before you can change your behaviour, habits or actions. I dedicate Chapters 7 through to 9 to this important work.

*** **Question 5:** What will you do to take you closer to your desired score? What you *choose* to do is not the same as what you *should* do. Notice how these two phrases feel different energetically. Choice feels light. 'Should' feels heavy. Let Future You choose, not your inner critic, perfectionist or people pleaser (more about them in Chapter 8).

Excitement vs. nervousness

Are you excited, hopeful and energised by all the possibilities ahead? Or nervous about creating Future You? Somewhere in between? Remember that the way you *choose* to think about this will partly determine your success. If you think, *This won't work for me*, it likely won't. I've found that my clients who say, 'This doesn't work' usually haven't tried or dedicated enough time to it. My clients who approach it with an open mind are often amazed at the clarity and insights they get. And the results. If you think, *I'm not quite sure, but I'll give it a go*, you're halfway there.

While the physiological responses to nervousness and excitement are similar (increased heart rate, faster and shallower breathing, dilated pupils, sweating) our *interpretation* of those responses depends on our perception of the situation, past experience and contextual and cultural factors. If we interpret the situation positively – *I'm excited* – we will experience excitement. If we perceive the situation as worrying or threatening, we'll *feel* nervous. We feel things as *we* are, not as *they* are.

Alison Wood Brooks, a behavioural research scientist who studies preperformance anxiety, wrote about her research in the *Harvard Business Review*:

> Research participants who were asked to give an impromptu three-minute talk scored *higher* on persuasiveness and confidence if they first said to themselves 'I am excited,' in comparison with those who said 'I am anxious' or explicitly tried to calm down.[10]

---

10 Wood Brooks, A, 'How to make use of your anxiety for positive results', *Harvard Business Review* (2013), https://hbr.org/2013/11/how-to-make-use-of-your-anxiety-for-positive-results, accessed 21 October 2024. Also see Wood Brooks, A, 'Get excited: Reappraising pre-performance anxiety as excitement', *Journal of Experimental Psychology: General*, 143/4 (2014), www.apa.org/pubs/journals/releases/xge-a0035325.pdf, accessed 21 October 2024

While we are commonly told to calm ourselves down before high-arousal situations, Wood's research suggests it's easier and more effective to shift from one high-arousal emotion (eg, anxiety) to another (eg, excitement) shortly before or during a task. Understanding that your physiological responses to excitement and nervousness are essentially the same can help reframe how you perceive those feelings. Choose your label wisely: which one is more likely to lead to success?

My top tip? Be excited about Future You!

At the beginning of this book, we identified some non-negotiable beliefs for being successful in your leadership life – whatever that means for you. In Case Studies 5 and 6, we will explore what happens when two people handle the same challenge or fear differently because of their beliefs about what is possible. Anna (Case Study 5) and Liz (Case Study 6) are leaders in two different organisations. They have different backgrounds and life experiences. Both fear giving presentations to large groups of people.

🔍 CASE STUDY 5: Anna

Anna decided not to apply for a promotion – for which she is supremely capable – as a more senior role would involve giving large conference speeches. Anna is a bold, courageous, purposeful and respected leader. She does not believe, however, that she will ever be able to deliver those big-group presentations.

Anna is making a choice that stems from the thoughts *I can't* and *I'm no good at this*, along with a fear of what *could* happen (eg, drying up, losing her thread, feeling exposed, shaking too much.) She lets her fear overpower her belief that she can change her situation, avoiding perceived failure. She told me, 'I can't change it at this stage. It's sad, but that's just how it is.'

Various well-meaning people in the past have suggested that Anna think positive, have a growth mindset, believe in herself or go on a course. Right now, however, suggestions like these are not going to cut it. Why? Because the only voice she's listening to is the fearful one in her head.

She may change her thoughts about presentations over time or she may not. There is no judgement here. We are all responsible for our own thoughts and decisions. The lesson here is to show empathy and compassion for ourselves (and people like Anna), whatever our choices.

🔎 CASE STUDY 6: Liz

Liz's first thoughts about giving big presentations were much like Anna's: *I'm no good at this.* 'I always get wobbly when I speak in a small group, so I end up waffling. A bigger group would be harder,' she told me. 'But equally, I know I've got to slay that dragon.' She spent time mapping out her version of Future You, seeing herself with a more senior job title. She visualised introducing herself with that new title. She started to feel excited about what could be possible for her.

Liz let her belief that she could change her situation overpower her fear and was open to working to overcome those fears. She volunteered to run part of a training session in a bigger group. 'I'm nervous, but excited-nervous,' she told me.

Those words – *excited, nervous* – are important. Remember that Liz can choose how her body interprets these feelings by consciously choosing how to label them. Before her first presentation, we practised together. I pushed her gently as we practised getting in the 'zone' beforehand, practising structure and delivery styles and the Q&A portion of the training session.

Liz told me afterwards, 'I presented the section we'd agreed on and did a piece I had not practised much. I had butterflies of excitement. It wasn't perfect and I know I have a long way to go to get comfortable with this, but I was pleasantly surprised and proud of myself.'

This is exactly how to align with Future You. Liz knew where she was going and got over one mental hurdle at a time by taking action even if she didn't think she was ready. Action leads to confidence, not the other way around. Confidence is cumulative.

We often make things we're afraid of huge and frightening, catastrophising about what-ifs, but the reality is rarely as bad as we imagine it will be. In this chapter, we discussed how mindfully choosing Future You thoughts is crucial to your success. In Chapter 7, we'll explore this further. First, your key takeaways.

Key takeaways

- Preparing to become Future You will require preparation and planning. Use the five questions in Activity 19 to bring your future self to life.

- 'I am excited' and 'I am nervous' have the same physiological responses, so do the 'scary' thing and it becomes less scary. Do the thing!

- Ask yourself, 'What would the best version of you want the you of today to do?' Then do it.

- The path from A to B is a voyage of discovery. That's why we're taking six months to get there.

7
Think About Your Thoughts

We now know how much our thoughts determine the way we show up as leaders and the results we get. In this chapter, we'll discuss in more depth how to turn unhelpful thoughts into helpful ones that help you succeed, get the results you want and align with Future You. We'll learn how our thoughts relate to our results, connecting the dots between what we choose to think or believe and the outcomes or results we get. I'll illustrate this with case studies from my clients Jack and Ed.

Thoughts on thoughts

According to a 2020 study conducted by a team of researchers from Queen's University in Canada, we have more than 6,000 thoughts daily.[11] These thoughts vary in duration or complexity from fleeting, sub-conscious notions to deeply thought-out solutions to complex problems.

Some of these are conscious thoughts: *I think it's time for a break*, or *I think I'll delegate this task to Simone*. Others are subconscious thoughts that exist below the surface. They may be influenced by current context, past experiences, conditioning, emotions or thought patterns. Subconscious thoughts can include deeply ingrained beliefs, fears, biases and memories that influence our behaviour without our being aware of them. Subconscious thoughts have become habitu-ated. We speak some of our thoughts out loud; others form part of our inner monologue. Whether conscious or subconscious, spoken or unspoken, every thought we have impacts our actions and results. Our thoughts impact how we feel, and vice versa.

Let's imagine you're at work right now. You've been working hard all day, deadlines pressing in, and you've got plenty more to do before the day is over. We can see the difference your thoughts make here: *I need a break; I'm tired. I'll go and have a cup of tea*, vs. *I need a break, but I've got to keep going as I can't let people down*. Your thoughts will lead you either to get a cuppa and come back feeling refreshed and clear-headed or

11 Tseng, J, and Poppenk, J, 'Brain meta-state transitions demarcate thoughts across task contexts exposing the mental noise of trait neuroticism', *Nature Communications*, 11/3480 (2020), www.nature.com/articles/s41467-020-17255-9, accessed 27 August 2024

to keep working and possibly make mistakes because of your tiredness. Thoughts like *I must keep going* or *I can't let people down* are examples of the type of habitual, reflexive thoughts we often have, regardless of the consequences. Remember, just because we *think* something doesn't make it true – especially when we do not consider the thought more deeply.

When you have thoughts like these, there are two insightful questions you can ask: *Why do I think this?* and *Is this a Future You thought?* No thought is right or wrong, but it helps to ask yourself which ones take you closer to Future You. Be curious about your thoughts. Ask yourself:

- Where did that thought come from?

- Do I believe this thought? Why?

- Do other people believe this? Why?

- What if the opposite thought were true?

I don't believe that thoughts are positive or negative, right or wrong. One thought might be 'right' for you today but 'wrong' for you tomorrow or in the long term. Once you bring your thoughts, helpful or otherwise, into your conscious awareness, you can decide what to do with them and separate the facts from the fiction.

'So how do I change my thoughts, Lynn?', I hear you ask.

Much of the time, we're unaware of our thoughts. We're on autopilot day in and day out, repeating the same behaviour patterns until we turn the autopilot off. Our brains always choose the easiest option, so we need to give them some better options to work with and reprogramme our mental GPS, which means, once again, reprogramming our neural pathways.

📑 CASE STUDY 7: Jake

I worked with Jake a couple of years ago. At the end of our coaching, he was headhunted by a competitor, given a big increase in salary and went off into the sunset.

Six months later, he got in touch again. 'Honestly, I'm starting to regret taking this job,' he told me. 'The organisation's a s**t show. I'm firefighting most of the time, and I spend my Saturdays trying to stay on top of things. My boss is losing patience – I think he might fire me.' Jake was not happy, but despite all of this, he decided to stick with it rather than walk away. I could see several thoughts playing on Jake's mind. You can probably feel his sense of helplessness and exhaustion, just as I did.

Top of Jake's list of 'hot', or worrying, thoughts was, *I think he might fire me.* That imagined threat was sending him into a state of fear – what we commonly describe as 'survival' or 'fight-or-flight' mode. In that state, Jake's brain could not do its best work. All his energy was used up trying to protect himself in the only ways he knew how: overworking and trying to stay in control.

His initial thought – *I might get fired* – made him feel helpless, on edge and jumpy. If *I just keep working*, he told himself, *I'll get on top of things sooner or later.* The result? He wasn't building the influence he wanted. He found it hard to focus most of the time. Things were taking too long. His team was rudderless. He was losing his confidence and doubting himself.

'What if it didn't have to be this way?' I asked him. (Hold onto that *what-if?*; it's a useful question in your toolbox.)

He was (unusually) lost for words. Jake goes swimming every Sunday, so I suggested he take the thought into the pool for some space time: *What if it doesn't have to be this way?*

For six months, we worked through the activities you've become familiar with in this book: carving out space, recognising time suckers, visualising his ideal future, examining helpful and unhelpful thoughts, looking at choices and taking small actions every day. He followed the process I've laid out in this book – the same process that you are going through now. Things became challenging for him a couple of times, but instead of working long hours to 'fix' them, he took some time away to get back on track. He even started swimming more often, as he got some of his best ideas during space time in the pool.

And no, he didn't get fired.

How thoughts affect outcomes

We cannot change every situation. But we can choose whether to accept the situation as it is or to do something else. Or we can choose to view the situation through a different lens. If we want something different, we need to focus on the things we can control, influence and change. That gives us agency and puts us in the driving seat. Whatever your starting point in life, your past experiences or current circumstances, there are three things you can change right now:

- Your thoughts and beliefs

- Your decisions

- Your actions and behaviour

What holds most of us back from the success we desire? Our thoughts and beliefs about what is possible for us. What *else*? We treat our thoughts, beliefs and perceptions as facts outside our control, blaming them for our circumstances. For example:

- The job market's terrible.

- This company doesn't value people.

- It's difficult to prioritise when there's so much to do.

- My boss doesn't care.

- I don't have time.

These thoughts describe our perception of a situation, but that doesn't make them true. 'The reality is', you say, but it's only *your* reality. Let's look at how the way you choose to perceive a situation can play out. In the following table, Leona and Hetal don't like their current job.

Anticipating success vs. avoiding failure

Perception	Avoiding failure: Leona	Anticipating success: Hetal
Leona disguises her thoughts as facts while Hetal acknowledges the more complex reality.	The job market's terrible.	There are fewer jobs than there used to be, but they are still out there.
Leona's thoughts keep her stuck while Hetal's move him forward.	There is no point even looking.	I can start looking tomorrow.
Both Leona and Hetal's thoughts lead to feelings and vice versa.	I feel despondent.	I feel cautiously optimistic.
Both Leona and Hetal's feelings lead to action or inaction.	I'll do nothing until the market improves.	I'll create a list of companies I want to work for, use my contacts, set up a meeting with a recruiter and update my CV.
Leona and Hetal's thoughts lead to different outcomes.	I'll stay in a job I hate while I wait it out.	I have set up two interviews.
Leona and Hetal's thoughts are self-fulfilling prophecies. We are what we believe.	The job market's terrible, so I won't get a job. I'm stuck here.	There are jobs out there. I act accordingly and get a new job.

As we've discussed, our thoughts, feelings, actions and outcomes are interconnected processes in our brains. Our thoughts tend to create self-fulfilling prophecies.

Activity 20 will help you examine how your thoughts, perceptions and feelings, along with how you act on them, will help you succeed. Activity 21 will show you how changing just one thought can make a big positive difference on the road to Future You.

💡 ACTIVITY 20: 'anticipate success' vs. 'avoid failure' check-in

1. Think of an important event that's coming up soon in your leadership life (eg, the board meeting on Tuesday, your upcoming one-on-one, your promotion interview, your project update presentation or the company restructure). On one line, write down a factual description of the scenario, situation or event. Note that statements like 'I'm too busy', 'My colleague is unhelpful' or 'They don't think I'm good enough' are not factual descriptions, but thoughts. 'I have ten things on my priority list' is a fact. Recognise the difference between opinion, perception and facts. A statement is a fact when you have hard evidence to prove it.

2. Anticipating success (as always), write down what a successful outcome would look like in whatever scenario you chose.

3. Write down all your thoughts about the outcome you want, and don't censor yourself. Do you think, *This will go well because...?* or *I know what to do to get there?* Or do you think the opposite? *This won't go well because...* or *It's always a nightmare.* In other words, are you anticipating success? Recognise the difference between the facts and your opinions, perceptions or thoughts. Remember that *this is where the gold lies.*

4. Write down your feelings. When you think about this scenario, do you feel worried, excited, bored, fearful? Whatever you feel, sit with it for a bit. Thoughts lead to feelings and vice versa. You may notice your thought first, *I'm not prepared so I feel anxious* or your feeling first *I feel anxious because I've not done enough preparation* (we'll cover this in more detail in Chapter 9).

Note: It doesn't matter whether you notice feelings or thoughts first. No thought is right or wrong, and no feeling is right or wrong. They're all essential data for you, and cultivating awareness and nonjudgemental curiosity about them is the first step to change.

5. Write down what actions you are likely to take right now that will help you achieve the successful outcome you outlined in Step 2. For example, if you are worried that you are not prepared enough for your meeting, you could plan to do some preparation to make you feel less anxious: *I can cancel that meeting on Thursday to give me prep time.*

ACTIVITY 21: Your thoughts create your reality

This activity is designed to help you notice how changing one thought can get you on the route to success. Recognising anticipate-success and avoid-failure thoughts is vital to achieving your desired future outcomes.

For this activity, choose a thought, perhaps one you noted in point 3 of the previous activity, and use these questions to shine a light on your thinking:

- Do you want to keep thinking this thought?
- Is this a Future You, anticipate-success thought?
- Is this an avoid-failure thought?
- Is this thought true? How do you know? Where's the proof?
- What are the consequences of sticking with this thought?
- What if the opposite thought were true? If it were, what would you do right now?
- What thought can you believe today that moves you one step closer to Future You?

You can do this activity anytime, anywhere. Start each day by focusing on what success looks like and generating the thoughts that help you achieve it, then prepare accordingly.

Realistic optimism vs. toxic positivity

Avoid-failure thoughts often lead to self-sabotage, avoidance, overthinking, analysis paralysis, making excuses and procrastination. These thoughts protect your ego, keeping it safe. Anticipate-success thoughts, on the other hand, are likelier to lead to the outcome you want. Even if you don't know immediately what reaching that outcome entails, when you anticipate success you'll take steps to find out.

Anticipating success should not be confused with toxic positivity, which occurs when we believe we should 'think positive' all the time, downplaying our emotions or experiences or ignoring risk. Denying the challenges of a situation is likely to lead to poor outcomes. Our beliefs about our own capacity and resilience influence how we cope with and approach those challenges, but we cannot just change our thoughts from *I'm not confident about this presentation* to *I'm super-confident about this presentation* in five minutes because we won't believe the new thought. It's too big a jump. If you're finding it hard to choose a thought that serves Future You, go for what I call 'optimistically realistic' thoughts such as:

- What if I *could* deliver a great presentation?

- I am open to the possibility that I *could* deliver an excellent presentation.

- I'm not where I want to be with the presentation *yet*, so I'll start with a mind map.

When you imagine what-ifs and are open to possibilities, you can identify your first step forward. When you use the word 'yet', you realise you have time to grow, change and do things that get you closer to where you want to be. It's also important to beware of the word 'should' when taking stock of your thoughts. 'Should' beliefs (eg, I should feel confident, but I'm not. What is wrong with me?) are generally unhelpful. 'Should' is a critical, disempowering word that implies you must do something simply because it's expected of you. Once you've taken your first small step, consider what your next anticipate-success thought might be. What action will you take because of that thought? Future You lies on the other side of your best thoughts.

📑 CASE STUDY 8: Ed

This case study covers a conversation I had with my client Ed. He had a one-on-one with his boss scheduled at 2pm the day of our conversation. His team had almost hit its sales target, but not quite. Ed knew his desired outcome: to showcase his achievements and get his boss's sign-off to hire a freelancer, but his thoughts were getting in the way. Let's look at them ('anticipate failure' thoughts are in italics): 'I haven't quite hit the target again and *I know she will be angry* even though it's only the second time in six months. I know we'd get there if we hire a freelancer for a couple of days, but my boss is always banging on about needing to save money, *so there doesn't seem to be any point. She'll say no. There's no point in asking*.'

Ed recognised *there's no point in asking* as his 'hot thought', but none of the italicised thoughts was a fact, even though

Ed talked as if they were. Ed was *feeling* disheartened about this upcoming conversation. He wanted to feel hopeful instead. He wrote down four thoughts that could help him get from disheartened to hopeful:

- I've reached the target most months and know I can do it.
- Last time we hired him, the freelancer got us through our backlog so we could focus on getting a new client – and we got two.
- Money is tight, but I can demonstrate a return on investment.
- Even if my boss says no, nothing ventured, nothing gained.

The first column of the following table lists thoughts that are 'helpful' to Ed's desired outcome – they're 'future Ed' thoughts. In the second column, he is already resigned to not getting what he wants.

Thoughts, feelings and actions

Anticipate success	Avoid failure
Thought	
My boss knows how much I've done to get close to the line, and I have an idea to help us reach or exceed.	My boss will tell me I've not done enough. She'll be angry.
Feeling	
I feel hopeful. If I can argue a strong enough case, my boss will like my idea and let me hire a freelancer.	I feel disheartened and nervous. I've got an idea, but I'm sure my boss won't like it because it involves investing in a freelancer. Last time I asked, she said no.

(Continued)

Anticipate success	Avoid failure
Potential action based on my thought and feeling	
I'll list the specific things that helped us get close to our target and put together a good business case for two days of the freelancer's time.	I'll do nothing. There is no point in asking for a freelancer; the answer will be 'no'. There's no money.
Potential outcome	
I get the freelancer on board, and we reach our target.	I don't get to hire the freelancer because I didn't ask, and I don't hit the target even though the team works flat-out.

As Ed indicated, nothing ventured, nothing gained. He showed up, prepared and improved his business case writing skills. His boss might have said no to his request, but the good news is that Ed did get sign-off to hire the freelancer for a couple of days. He reworked his business case, and his team hit their target that month.

Will you always get what you want if you anticipate success? No, but that's OK. There's no 'failure' when you anticipate success. You show up as the best version of yourself, and you always learn something. When all your energy is spent on 'avoiding failure', you shrink, go into hiding and stay stuck. There's no growth there – only regrets.

'If I've had these unhelpful thoughts forever, can I still change them?'

Yes, you can.

'Can I even eliminate the negative commentator in my head?'

Yes. You can choose whether to listen to that commentator or do something else. In Chapter 8, you'll get up-close and personal with your inner critic. And learn how to tame it. First, your key takeaways.

Key takeaways

- Be conscious of your thoughts. Explore them. Be curious about them. Ask, *Why do I think that?*

- Challenge the thoughts that keep you stuck: *I can't do this, I don't have time, It's too difficult.* Is any of this true, or is it all opinion? Show yourself the evidence.

- Anticipating success can help you to find the aspects of a situation that you can control, while avoiding failure sets you up to do nothing to address your problems.

- Be careful not to confuse anticipating success with toxic positivity. Anticipating success is a mindset of realistic optimism, in which you open yourself to the possibility that you can achieve your goal. Toxic positivity, on the other hand, means you might brush off or avoid problems rather than facing them. The best way to deal with challenges is to put on your anticipate-success hat first and then do the necessary preparation.

- Notice any thoughts that start with 'should'. They can weigh us down rather than take us closer to Future You.

8
Tame Your Inner Critic

The inner critic is that niggly internal dialogue that judges, criticises, demeans or sabotages you. It is the voice that whispers in your ear, 'Who are you to think you can do that?' or, 'You'll never pull that off' or, 'You'll never be as good as she is'. This voice tells you you're not worthy. It tells you not to speak up in case you make an idiot of yourself. It often uses 'must', ' should' and 'can't'.

The inner critic gives voice to your inner people pleaser, perfectionist, chimp and saboteur, along with your imposter syndrome. It can include the critical voice of a parent or significant figure in your life. It can govern your thoughts, behaviours, actions and results *if you let it*. The inner critic fills you with old, habitual thoughts that don't align with Future You.

Recognise it? Me too. Nearly everyone – presidents, CEOs, elite athletes and A-listers – has an inner critic. It may be present in one part of our lives but not another. It may disappear for ages and then sneak right back in again. Most inner critics have a typical script that plays out in certain situations or with certain people. My inner critic, for example, used to be particularly active around older, more senior men. One of my clients, a proud Glaswegian, says hers shows up when she's with 'posh Southerners'.

The inner critic often feels so normal that we don't notice it's leading the way. In this chapter, you're going to get up-close and personal with your inner critic. I'll give you some practical ways to tame that critic and find your inner coach, cheerleader or supporter. I use the word *tame* deliberately, because I don't believe you can eliminate your inner critic. It'll still pop up uninvited occasionally, but once you know what you're up against, you can face it with your anticipate-success hat on and Future You in mind. These days, when mine pops up, I say, 'Oh, it's that thing again', and send it back into hibernation.

The inner critic and the inner cheerleader

The inner critic and the ego

I first came across the notion of the inner critic in Timothy Gallwey's *The Inner Game of Tennis*. Gallwey, who was a tennis coach in the 1970s, asserts that inside every tennis player are two voices, belonging to what he describes as 'Self 1' and 'Self 2'. Self 1 gives a running commentary on everything that Self 2 does, and it's often critical: 'You're too slow', 'You'll never be able to beat her' and so on.

Self 1, the inner critic, is neither kind nor (well, rarely) truthful, though it would tell you otherwise. 'I'm only trying to protect you from harm and danger,' it whines. To a small extent, it has a point. Your brain's first priority is to keep you alive, so it focuses on avoiding pain, seeking pleasure and saving energy. That's great news for our cave-dwelling ancestors fighting or fleeing the woolly mammoth. It's not so great for us, however, when 'avoiding pain' means avoiding the discomfort of speaking up and 'saving energy' means staying on autopilot even though it's not getting the results we want. It can seem difficult to stop and think and easier to keep going, but you now know what happens when that pattern continues for too long: Future You starts to drift away.

Gallwey perfectly sums up the inner critic: 'The opponent within one's own head is more formidable than the one on the other side of the net.'[12] In other words, you are the biggest obstacle to your success. Only you can prevent Future You from emerging. Gallwey's equation, performance = potential − interference (interference being the inner critic) is a great way to remind yourself that you'll only align with Future You when you stop letting Self 1 choose the path.

Let's get to know your inner critic so you know what you're dealing with, starting with Activity 22.

💡 ACTIVITY 22: Describe your inner critic

Describe your inner critic in as much detail as you can. You can draw it or write a poem or story about it – whatever helps you to bring it to mind. What does it look like, and when does it appear? What does it say, and how does it sound? How do you feel when it is with you? Maybe your inner critic has a name: 'Oh, it's Mabel trying to muscle in again.' Perhaps it appears as a devil on your shoulder or a ball of wool in your stomach.

Visualising your inner critic can make it easier to banish, at least temporarily. You can shrink it, turn the volume down, put it in a box or move it to another room far away. You can unravel the ball of wool or spit it out like a hairball. My client Janine described her inner critic as a gremlin-faced old man with no name.

---

12 Gallwey, TW, *The Inner Game of Tennis: The ultimate guide to the mental side of peak performance* (Pan, 2015)

The image was crystal-clear to her. When she saw it in her mind, she could pause what she was doing and metaphorically move the man out of sight – and out of mind.

Learned beliefs

Freud described the 'superego' as the component of our personality made up of internalised ideas or scripts we acquire from an early age. Those scripts come mainly from our family of origin – parents or caregivers – but it's also shaped by our education, religion (Catholic guilt is real – ask my mum), cultural norms, ethnicity, country of birth, gender, region, community.

We often swallow whole the things we learn in our early days and don't question them in later life. How often have you said something and said to yourself, 'I sound just like my mother (or father)?' Or do you go the opposite way? 'I never want to be like my parents.' Maybe your mother always said, 'Pull yourself together', so you find it hard to open up or ask for help at work. Maybe your father was never happy unless you got straight As, so you believe that only perfection is good enough. This makes perfectionism into our default position, leading to exhaustion and micromanaging. Maybe you were taught not to show off, so the thought of being in the limelight or winning an award is excruciating for you. We pick up these subliminal messages early in life and swallow them whole.

My father was opinionated and 'always right'. He wasn't interested in debate or curious about anybody else's views. My mother sat back and let him get on with it, often having to apologise to people after he'd stepped over the line. He could be moody for hours at a time, and we all learned to tiptoe around him until he returned to good spirits. My mother never said it, but the message I got was, 'Tiptoe around conflict. Appease. Stay quiet. Don't share your opinions if they're "different".' That way, I learned, you survive, save energy and avoid pain or conflict.

How do you think those learned beliefs and behaviours showed up in my early leadership life? I struggled to speak up with more senior people (particularly men), have honest conversations, stand up for myself and share my opinions. I became anxious during heated debates.

I do not tell you this as an exercise in blame or self-pity. My parents, along with everybody else, have inner critics, learned behaviours and scripts, too. I also learned a lot of great stuff from my parents. Both came from low-income families and won grammar school places, but their families had no money for university education. There were no student loans in those days. My parents were keen to pull out all the stops so we had opportunities to learn and travel.

My mum was the kindest person I knew. My dad was the life and soul of the party and generous to his team at work. He was also a great negotiator with a strong anticipate-success belief that you can almost always get a cheaper price if you ask. Those beliefs helped me immensely in my travel industry career, where good negotiating skills were essential.

My point is, we've got to learn from the past, then move on. Learning from the past and living in the present helps us to shape our future selves with anticipation and joy. Yet, too often, we get stuck in the past, letting previous 'bad' experiences cloud our judgement.

CASE STUDY 9: Cara

My client Cara was upset. She thought she'd nail her interview, but in her words, it was 'a disaster'. She didn't get the promotion she wanted. She waffled, panicked and struggled to answer the questions. She told me she checked her email just before the interview and got bad news about a client contract, which made her distracted and worried. 'I've lost my confidence,' she told me. She had another interview scheduled for the next month, and her overriding thought was, 'I don't want to screw up again.' What a hot thought that is!

When we go into something thinking, 'I mustn't screw this up', our brain focuses on the 'screw up' bit, making us fearful, anxious and hypervigilant. In this state, using all her energy to 'not screw up', Cara can't do her best thinking. Her executive brain will not work as well as it could.

We spent some time developing her confidence for the next interview. When we did some 'Interview Future You' visualisation exercises, Cara saw herself answering interview questions succinctly and showcasing her talent and experience. She chose the mantra 'I am showcasing me at my best' and put it on a Post-It note on her computer screen to get her RAS working.

She kept the hour before the interview free to do some singing to energise herself. She also re-read a recent email from a customer thanking her for her great work. Though some nervousness crept in on interview day, she called it 'excitement' (see Chapter 6, 'Excitement vs. nervousness')

I also gave her this tip: never, ever check emails or texts just before doing something important. Instead, spend that time channelling Future You. Reframe your nervousness as excitement or do something that helps you feel relaxed and confident. Anticipate success and get in the zone.

Cara was still waiting to hear whether she got the job at the time of writing. Either way, though, she felt she'd done her best and left her inner critic under the bed, where she put him before she left the house.

Either/or thinking

One of my earliest coaching contracts (I'd not been out of training that long) was with a super-talented man in his early 30s who had been promoted to the board of trustees for an insurance brokerage based in London. He'd been raised to believe that obedience and deference to authority figures were non-negotiable. This made it hard for him, the youngest man in the office, to challenge the older men in trustee meetings. *I must respect their wisdom and experience*, he thought, though, of course, they weren't always wise, and he knew it. His belief was, *I can either be respectful and say nothing or be disrespectful and speak up*.

I call this type of thinking, where we limit our thoughts to two narrow options, 'either/or thinking'. When we notice our limiting either/or thoughts, we need to reframe them as 'and' thoughts. When my client asked himself, *How can I be respectful and honest* and *say what's on my mind?*, he was able to find the courage to speak up.

💡 ACTIVITY 23: Evaluating beliefs

Think about a belief that you hold. Choose one that often plays out using 'must', 'should', 'ought', or similar phrases. Some of these beliefs might be helpful on the path to Future You, but others won't. Some are helpful in one situation but not another. The key is to know the difference; these questions can help:

- How does the belief play out daily in your life and work?
- What benefits does the belief hold for your leadership?

- Where might the belief get in the way of Future You?
- Are you avoiding anything because of the belief?
- Are you achieving anything because of the belief?
- What might make the belief more helpful, empowering or constructive?

Remember, unpicking your beliefs is not an exercise in blame or regret. This exercise is designed to clarify the background and context of your belief and will give you some 'a-ha!' moments.

🔍 CASE STUDY 10: Victoria

Victoria's core belief about herself was *I don't do conflict*. She told herself, *I'm terrible when it comes to difficult conversations*, using this belief as a strategy to avoid dealing with a poor performer on her team. Meanwhile, the rest of her team were desperate for her to bite the bullet.

Through coaching, Victoria came to understand that *I don't do conflict* is an avoidance strategy thought, not a fact. She found a belief more in keeping with her leadership role: *I set clear expectations because I believe in excellence*. With that belief in mind, she was able to plan and prepare for her difficult conversation with the poor performer. We worked on visualising the conversation and practising it out loud. Working through a few different scenarios and what-ifs helped her feel grounded, confident and purposeful. (You'll find my 'Confident conversations checklist' at www.effortlessleaders.com/lynn-scott-leader-unlocked.)

Switching off your inner critic

Once you have a clear picture of your inner critic, the next step is to pay attention and recognise when it is in the room. Many inner critic thoughts are subconscious. They tend to become default thoughts that can drive you into a pessimistic spiral of negative self-talk. Instead, I want you to keep anticipating success and choosing Future You thoughts.

As I wrote this chapter, my inner critic popped by to say hello. I suddenly felt tired, grumpy and unfocused, and I wanted to scroll through nonsense on social media. 'You're never going to hit your word count today', my inner critic said. 'You're failing' became, *'You're a failure'*. The irony that my inner critic appeared when I was writing about it is not lost on me.

Recognising my inner critic was my cue to change it. When that 'you're a failure' thought kicks in, I leave my desk. I go outside, get some air or do some stretches (I keep my exercise mat on my office floor to keep my RAS on-side). I can turn the volume down on my inner critic until it is nothing but a whisper, then falls silent. By changing my physiological state, I can access Future Me. The voice of my inner coach or cheerleader becomes louder. She won't accept those ridiculous stories my inner critic spouts.

🔍 CASE STUDY 11: Debbie

'I'm a terrible decision maker,' Debbie said when we first met. 'I'm thinking of applying for a new job I've seen advertised, but I can't decide whether it will be a good move or whether it will be going from frying pan to fire. I just can't decide whether to apply or wait until I know what I want to do. Or maybe I should just wait until a promotion comes up? I don't know.'

She had believed that 'terrible decision maker' story for so long, that it became a self-fulfilling prophecy. She was stuck ruminating, doing nothing.

I asked her, 'If you were the best decision maker in the world, what would you do right now?'

She knew the answer right away: 'I could just apply, couldn't I?' After our call, she went off and did just that. She challenged her belief and removed the label she'd given herself. She knew exactly what to do.

Define yourself as the person you want to become: *I am someone who can make decisions without overthinking*, or *I am someone who can evict my inner critic when it appears.* The more you try these new identity beliefs on for size, the more you become Future You. Stick with the *I'm a terrible decision maker* script, and that's who you'll be.

'What about my feelings, Lynn? Sometimes they overwhelm me. What can I do?'

I'm glad you asked, because that is where we're going in Chapter 9. First, your key takeaways.

Key takeaways

- Nearly everyone has an inner critic that puts them down or makes them doubt themselves. Often, its voice is so constant that we don't even notice it is driving our decisions.

- The inner critic has an evolutionary purpose. Being able to recognise danger or threat was a survival mechanism that kept our ancestors alive. For us, however, it's rarely our physical survival that's at risk, it's our ego. Say 'thank you' to your inner critic for its good intentions, but it is no longer needed in your life. Bye, bye.

- To switch your inner critic off, always consciously define yourself alongside Future You. Often, the biggest battle is your inner critic vs. Future You. Always stick with Future You.

- Define yourself always as the person you want to become. 'I am someone who…'.

9
Untangle Emotional Triggers

We've discussed at length our thoughts and how they affect outcomes, but what about emotions? Our emotional state strongly impacts the quality of our thinking and, therefore, our effectiveness. It used to be said that our thoughts create our feelings. Many neuroscientists now challenge that view, however, and believe that thoughts and emotions are deeply intertwined; they influence and shape each other. The brain constructs emotions based on several factors, including context, culture and experience. Still, many people are so 'in their heads' that they miss critical emotional data, losing the opportunity to learn from them.

Feelings at work

Organisations are full of feelings. In fact, they are hotbeds of emotion. There's the leader frozen in fear whenever she hears perceived criticism, the leader who feels deeply inadequate but chooses to mask it with bravado and the team member who feels angry and resentful because she thinks her boss doesn't trust her. There are collective worries about restructures or redundancies, unspoken resentments within teams, anxieties about being replaced by AI and conflicts between departments.

Emotions are contagious. Even if you think you can hide them, they tend to leak. The more senior your position, the more visible your behaviour becomes and the more people will tune into your mood and interpret what they think you're feeling. This can be dangerous territory if it means nobody tells you the truth or dares to contradict you. A team of fearful or disengaged people will never do its best work. Many leaders who want to be seen as confident and competent also struggle to be vulnerable with their teams. They may understand the importance of acknowledging past mistakes, acknowledging that they don't have all the answers and being honest about what they are doing to improve their performance, but still struggle to do it. Perhaps those leaders have a strong inner critic that tells them not to be 'weak'. Or a belief that they 'should' have all the answers.

Feelings leak

Hiding your feelings doesn't mean they go away. If your boss shouts at you, you may be furious, but you probably dare not stand your ground. Instead, you may take your anger out on your partner when you get home or suppress your anger for so long that it starts to affect your physical or mental health. You may choose unhealthy coping strategies. You may grow so used to feeling overwhelmed that it becomes the norm, and you give up trying to reduce your stress. Left unchecked, this can lead to burnout. We struggle to be collaborative, productive or decisive in this fight-or-flight state.

For years, I believed that I couldn't control my feelings. I hid my feelings from others and pushed down the feelings I didn't want to feel in the hope that they would go away (they didn't). We rarely acknowledged or talked about feelings in my family, so I had no clue how to self-regulate. I also believed that other people could make me feel happy, sad, angry and so on – in other words, they were in control, not me. This is simply not true. To paraphrase Eleanor Roosevelt, 'Nobody can make you feel *anything* without your permission'.

We can be emotionally triggered at any time, reacting to situations without thinking. 'I couldn't stop myself,' you may say. You may use all your energy trying not to feel your emotions until your anger, frustration or upset pops like a champagne cork – but without the celebratory bubbles. I don't believe that being emotionally triggered is a bad thing as long as you use it as an opportunity to recognise and clean up thoughts, beliefs or opinions that don't align with Future You. (You can find my emotional triggers exercise in the resource library at www.effortlessleaders. com/lynn-scott-leader-unlocked.)

Fear of rejection, in particular, can lead us to stifle or ignore our emotions, leading to emotional leakage. Rejection can feel unbearable, and many of us try to avoid it at all costs. Millennia ago, when rejection from the tribe meant near-certain death, that avoidance strategy *was* lifesaving. As we discussed in Chapter 8, our brains don't know the difference between protecting us from mortal danger (fleeing the woolly mammoth) and protecting our ego. It responds in the same way to both.

What's the result? Often, it's regret: you agree to something you don't believe in, say yes instead of no, hold back difficult feedback, make unkind comments to a colleague, lose your temper in a meeting and regret it. When we act from fear of rejection, everything *feels* more difficult.

Navigating emotional responses

How can you manage your emotions rather than be overwhelmed by them? Emotional regulation does not mean suppressing emotions because, paradoxically, suppression can increase those emotions. Regulation means mindfully choosing how to respond to our emotions – respond, not react. When your brain is tired, it's harder to regulate your emotions. This is one of the many reasons why it's important to prioritise space time in your working life.

Of course, you don't have to stifle or ignore your emotions now, because you have your pause button. It can help you leave a space between stimulus and response, allowing you to mindfully choose a Future You response instead of a knee-jerk, fight-or-flight one. Rejection and other challenges will happen. The great thing about anticipate-success beliefs is that we know we can learn from them rather than going into a doom loop.

One way to become more familiar with your emotions is to 'name the emotion to tame it'. This expression was coined by Dr Dan Siegel, a professor of psychiatry at the University of California, Los Angeles, School of Medicine whose research suggests that naming our feelings out loud reduces their intensity.[13] Once we're aware of the feeling, we can cognitively control it. How familiar are you with what you're feeling? Let's find out with Activity 24.

> ☀️ **ACTIVITY 24: See the emotion, name the emotion, don't be the emotion**
>
> Stop everything right now. Describe how you're feeling, naming the specific emotions you currently

---

13   Siegel, D, 'Name it to tame it' (2014), www.youtube.com/watch?v=ZcDLzppD4Jc, accessed 21 August 2024

feel. Naming emotions allows us to step back and decide what our feelings are telling us. For example, you might say, 'I feel uncertain. I don't want to feel uncertain.' Knowing that you feel uncertain allows you to consider why you feel that way.

It also allows you to consider how you might change your thoughts so you feel different. How can you cognitively control your feelings? For example, you might feel uncertain because you've been telling yourself that an upcoming meeting will be a nightmare. Ask yourself, 'If I was to anticipate success instead, how might that change my feeling?'

If you practise regularly tuning into your feelings, you'll become much more aware of them and more able to self-regulate in the moment.

Self-regulation techniques

Many people hold tension in their shoulders, back, jaw or stomach. They may want to speak up, for example, but their throat feels tight, and they literally lose their voice. This type of physiological discomfort can be a signal of dysregulated or unacknowledged emotions. When you recognise these feelings, try these techniques to bring yourself back under control:

1. Recognising and naming your feelings puts you in control. You can decide how to interpret your physical sensations.

2. Changing your physiological state can change how you feel. Fifteen minutes of activity – stretching, walking about, chair yoga – is all you need to feel different.

3. Sensory activities can also help you self-regulate, shifting your focus away from overwhelming or unhelpful thoughts. Exposure to sunlight can stimulate serotonin, a neurotransmitter that contributes to feelings of well-being. Simple sensory experiences like walking barefoot can release endorphins, called 'feel-good' hormones. Touching different fabrics or hugging someone you love work, too. If you've got a dog or a cat to stroke, you already know how soothing that can be.

One of my clients asked me recently, 'Why am I so angry with everyone?' When we explored further, she realised she was angry that people weren't doing what she expected. We dug a bit further, and it became clear she'd been somewhat ambiguous in her expectations. If we hadn't focused on that anger, that would still be a blind spot for her. She didn't want to feel angry; she wanted to feel calm and understood. Once she understood her anger, the ball was in her court. To paraphrase Siegel, we can *see* the emotion; we don't have to *be* the emotion.[14] Knowing that we can choose how we want to feel in any situation is powerful.

---

14 Siegel, D, '12 revolutionary strategies to nurture your child's developing mind, survive everyday parenting struggles, and help your family thrive', Dr Dan Siegel, https://drdansiegel.com/whole-brain-child-handouts, accessed 23 September 2024

🔍 CASE STUDY 12: Dan

Dan felt under pressure. For the first time in a year, he wasn't meeting his sales targets. He told himself he was a bad role model for his team and was uptight every time he spoke to a potential client. When we explored these feelings, Dan realised that, rather than anticipating success, he was trying to avoid failure. This made him sound pushy, needy and desperate. Do you want to buy from a pushy, needy, desperate person? Me neither. That type of energy repels. It doesn't attract.

Dan didn't need sales training or better skills. This wasn't a knowledge or competence issue. He'd been trained by some of the best salespeople in his industry. He just wanted to *feel* different (ie, not uptight.)

He imagined and created a mental movie of Future Dan, who was calm, open, relaxed and connected to his potential clients. He pictured a meeting of equals, where he could hear the potential client's concerns, slow down, ask questions and connect as one human being to another. More importantly, Future Dan knew he would be OK even if the customer said 'Thanks but no thanks', rather than taking it as a sign of failure.

Though being unattached to the outcome of sales meetings felt like a mountain to climb, Dan got to work. He put in place some short daily relaxation practices before changing anything else. He allowed himself more time before sales calls to get into the zone and afterwards to reflect. After a couple of weeks, being relaxed and at ease started to become his new normal. Unsurprisingly, more customers started to say 'yes', and even when they didn't, Dan could put the 'no' into perspective and not let it destroy the rest of his day.

Anyone who works in sales knows how overwhelming and personal rejection can feel if we choose to let it. Being comfortable with discomfort or disappointment is a tremendous gift. You can learn from it and move on, knowing that brighter things lie ahead.

🔍 CASE STUDY 13: Kathy

Kathy spoke with me about a colleague she was struggling with at work. She asked me a lot of questions like, 'Should I do this?' and 'Can I say that?'

I asked her to pause and tell me what she was feeling. She considered for quite a while. 'I don't know,' she said eventually. She sat with the question for a while longer, then touched her shoulders and said, 'I feel heavy.' She had the weight of the world on her shoulders, and it showed.

We did some experiments to help her connect with what was happening in her body – the all-important data she hadn't been paying attention to. What would it be like if a little bit of the weight came off her shoulders? A little bit more? Once the metaphorical weight was lifted, she could think more clearly about how to handle her colleague. She felt lighter.

The workplace can feel like an emotional minefield, particularly when we do not have emotional regulation skills. Recognising and naming our emotions makes them easier to control, allowing us to move on to solving problems. In Chapter 10, we will build on what we've learned so far and focus on building leadership confidence. First, your key takeaways.

Key takeaways

- Feelings do not disappear when we disregard or suppress them. Instead, they seep into our actions, leaking out at inopportune times.

- Feelings are valuable data. We can choose what to do with our feelings based on a few variables. No feeling is wrong, but it's important to be able to regulate feelings that are not healthy or helpful to Future You.

- Naming the feeling can enable us to reduce its intensity. Pausing to consider how we feel provides an opportunity to manage our response to challenging or uncomfortable emotions.

- Recognising your feelings, changing your physiological state and engaging in sensory activities can shift your mood and help you to self-regulate.

10
Confidence From Your Core

*H*ow *can I be more confident?*

Most of the leaders I work with say they want 'more confidence'. That goal is vaguer than it seems because there are many types of confidence. There's flashy, trained-within-an-inch-of-your-life confidence, superficial confidence that hides insecurity and confidence that results when people speak truth to power from deep within their core.

Confidence from your core

I tell my clients they need to get specific. 'I want to be more confident at speaking with impact', they may say, or, 'I lack confidence and conviction in the boardroom'. They may want more confidence sharing their vision or direction or setting boundaries and saying no. They may want more confidence to ask clearer, succinct questions rather than simply filling the space. I imagine you're saying, 'They'll gain confidence in these areas if they believe they can and take consistent action to build their confidence day by day.' If so, congratulations on applying what you've learned so far! You're correct: confidence is cumulative.

In this chapter, we will discuss confidence and how it differs from self-esteem and arrogance and we'll explore why both competence *and* confidence are essential for leaders. I'll debunk some common myths about confidence. We'll also complete four activities that build on the Future You work you've already done and create your confidence action plan.

What is confidence?

The word 'confidence' comes from the Latin *fidere*, which means 'to trust'; in other words, self-confidence is about trusting yourself. It comes from deep within your core. That's why we've been doing the work on your thoughts. Being clear about who you want to be and how you will get there – and anticipating that you will succeed – are fundamental to growing confidence. You must trust your ability to learn, change and improve with experience and practice. You must trust that you know enough even if you don't know *everything*; who does?

In his book *The Confident Mind*, Dr Nate Zinsser describes confidence as 'a sense of certainty about your ability that allows you to bypass conscious thought and execute unconsciously.'[15] I love this definition because it perfectly describes how I feel when I'm in flow. Whatever I'm doing feels effortless. My inner critic is hibernating, and I'm absorbed in what I'm doing or wholly connected to the people with me. I'm sure you have times when you're in flow, too. People might watch you and say, 'You make it look so easy', or 'You're a natural' – but I'd bet you've put in hours of practice over weeks, months or years to make it look effortless.

---

15 Zinsser, N, *The Confident Mind: A battle-tested guide to unshakable performance* (Penguin Books, 2023)

Confidence vs. self-esteem

Confidence and self-esteem are two different qualities with different requirements and functions. Self-esteem is related to your sense of self and identity. Improving it means learning to accept and love yourself as you are whilst also knowing that Future You is something you're moving towards from a place of possibility, not lack. People with high self-esteem love themselves unconditionally. They know self-worth doesn't improve with money, status, external validation or being the best in the world at something. If you constantly struggle with your sense of worth, however outwardly successful you are, there will be some reasons for this.[16] You can't change your past, but you can shape your future. The more you say, 'I'm not confident', the more it becomes a self-fulfilling prophecy. If you're confident in one area, you can cultivate confidence in another if you want to (and you must *want* to), because your confidence muscle is already in place. In this chapter, we're going to strengthen it.

Strengthening your confidence takes effort. We're sometimes impatient to get from A to B without putting in the work. This doesn't work because building confidence in a particular area is a marathon, not a sprint. It's enough to focus on being 1% better than

---

16 *Note:* This book focuses specifically on building self-confidence in your leadership role using the strategies I share with my coaching clients every day. If you want to improve your self-esteem in other areas of your life, you may consider working with a coach or a trained therapeutic practitioner in those areas.

you were yesterday, whatever anybody else does. I'm a confident executive coach. Others describe me as intuitive and direct, and I use those qualities to help my clients align with their future selves. I don't say this to boast, but to illustrate how far I've come since my early days of coach training. In those days, I had so much mind chatter I could barely focus on the person sitting in front of me, so fearful was I of failure. If I'd let those avoid-failure thoughts take over, I probably would have given up years ago. Somehow I believed that there was a Future Me coach emerging and stuck with it, trusting the process as I went along. And she continues to emerge.

Confidence vs. arrogance

The difference between confident and arrogant leadership is huge. Arrogance is self-importance, superiority and lack of care for others. Arrogant behaviour is often a defence mechanism that masks feelings of inadequacy, lack and deep insecurity. An arrogant person wants to protect their ego at all costs. True confidence, on the other hand, comes from self-belief, respect for others and comfort in your skin. True confidence is abundant. A confident leader helps others grow their confidence, recruits brilliant people and lets them get on with the job.

Still, sometimes leaders say, 'If I'm too confident, people might think I'm arrogant.' Let's consider that. Think of a confident colleague you trust. How does their confidence appear or play out? What do you admire about them? Think about how they carry themselves, make you feel, ask questions or move discussions in the right direction. Do you consider them arrogant? Probably not. This is because *confidence smiles; arrogance smirks.*

CONFIDENCE   **ARROGANCE**

Confidence vs. arrogance

Confidence vs. competence

Competence and confidence are not the same, but leaders need both. No amount of competence, which refers to skill level, will make up for a lack of confidence. I'm sure you know someone talented, intelligent, gifted or knowledgeable who regrets letting a lack of confidence hold them back. Likewise, bucketloads of confidence and a lack of competence, knowledge or expertise can lead to disaster. Imagine the havoc a confident and incompetent pilot or brain surgeon could wreak. People who overestimate their abilities may be entitled, domineering and focused on their own needs at the expense of everybody else. They often lack empathy and self-awareness.

The bottom line? You need both to get to Future You. The good news is, you already know what you have to do: the more you practise, the more competent and confident you will become. You can grow your confidence regardless of your starting point in life. To help you do this, later in this chapter we will create a confidence action plan. First, though, let's examine some myths about confidence.

Confidence myths

Myth 1: Confidence is innate

Confidence is not a fixed trait that we are born with. It's not genetic. It fluctuates depending on circumstances, life events and, as we've seen, our feelings and thoughts about ourselves. We can develop and improve our confidence through awareness, working on our thoughts and feelings and 'doing the thing' even when we don't feel ready.

This myth extends to 'confident people'. We often assume that confident people are confident in every aspect of their lives, but it's not true. Your CEO may be supremely confident talking about budget projections but less confident giving performance feedback to a team member. Almost everyone has an inner critic that pops up from time to time even if they might mask it well.

Myth 2: Extraverts are more confident than introverts

Confidence is not synonymous with extraversion. Extraverts often appear more confident than introverts because they are more outwardly social. Sometimes this means they are more likely to be promoted to senior leadership roles than competent introverts.

The truth is, extraversion and introversion do not come from confidence. Rather, they are related to our source of energy. Extraverts feel energised by social stimulation. For them, meeting new people and attending social gatherings are invigorating. Introverts, on the other hand, are energised by time alone, introspection and thinking. They find social gatherings in large doses exhausting. Confidence comes from being comfortable with who you are, regardless of your social preferences. Extraverts may struggle with confidence, and introverts can have lots of it.

Myth 3: You've got to fake it to make it

The jury's out on this one. Some people swear by 'fake it to make it' as a strategy. I suspect that these people see 'faking it' as something similar to anticipating success. They behave as though they will be successful, which gives them confidence. True confidence comes from our core, and we can strengthen our confidence muscles daily.

Personally, the word 'fake' doesn't sit well with me because it implies behaving in a way that contradicts our beliefs. This type of behaviour may make us feel inauthentic and uncomfortable, and people may sense that our energy is 'off' in some way. None of these inspire confidence.

📑 CASE STUDY 14: Suzi

Suzi liked to lead calmly and quietly. She was warm and thoughtful, but she believed that to be heard and respected by her (mainly) male peers, she *should* speak loudly and often, like they did.

Suzi was conflicted. Does she change her beliefs or adapt her behaviour? Does she do neither or both? This type of thinking, where we feel we 'should' act in a way that does not align with our beliefs, leads to cognitive dissonance, not confidence. To gain confidence, Suzi needed to find a way to restore her cognitive harmony.

I reminded her that either/or thinking, like *I can either be calm or shout to be heard*, keeps us stuck. Instead, she used 'and': *I can be calm and be heard without shouting*. That's the anticipate-success way.

Suzi asked her CEO for some tips on being heard, explaining the problem. He was mortified and recognised he'd contributed to her challenge. At the next meeting, he sought out Suzi's views, announcing that meetings would benefit from more thoughtful contributions and less shouting. (Well, he called it 'less d**k waving'.)

Myth 4: Confident people never doubt themselves

This myth is easy to bust. Almost everyone experiences self-doubt. Confidence does not mean never experiencing doubt; it means believing in your ability to overcome that doubt.

Myth 5: Confident people are loud and assertive

Some confident people are outspoken and express themselves loudly and energetically. Others demonstrate it through calm, listening and gravitas. Some people can do both. Calmly confident leaders often bring a sense of assurance and certainty, while outspoken confident leaders can inspire and motivate others. Confidence comes in many forms. Authentic Future You confidence, whatever form it takes, will excite and inspire you.

Myth 6: Confidence requires feedback

While we all appreciate feedback, valuing ourselves based on other people's opinions puts us in a state of constant alert. Believing you're only good enough if others say you are leads to a fragile, easily shaken sense of confidence. As the saying goes, confidence does not ask, 'Will they like me?' It says, 'I'll be fine if they don't'. (See Chapter 8 for a deeper understanding of where this need for external validation comes from and what you can do about it.)

The confidence action plan

You already know about visualising or imagining your future self, anticipating success, and consistently taking steps to get there. You know that action from a place of solid belief leads to confidence, not the other way around. Continuing to work on Future You thoughts and taking incremental steps will set you up for success.

This is where your confidence action plan comes in, which will include five steps:

- **Step 1:** Choose one area of your life where you want more confidence (see Activity 27). Incremental improvement is the goal, so it's important to focus your efforts on just one specific area that aligns with Future You. Once you are confident in this area, you can choose another and repeat the process as many times as you like.

- **Step 2:** Ensure your environment – location, people, sights, sounds, smells, tastes, sensations etc – supports you and your goals. Surround yourself with supporters and kind truthtellers, not naysayers or energy vampires. Spend time in places that energise and inspire you.

- **Step 3:** Engage a colleague, mentor or coach to help you – someone who believes in you, has your back and won't tolerate your excuses. This person will work with you through any challenges that arise, encouraging and pushing you when you need it.

- **Step 4:** Anticipate success. Use what-if questions to guide and inspire you, one step at a time. Ask yourself, *What if I could grow confidence in this area? What would I do?* Remember, confidence is cumulative. You will grow with each step, your confidence muscles getting stronger.

- **Step 5:** Visualise a confident Future You every day. Connect with them personally. What makes them so confident? How do they carry that confidence, and how does their behaviour reflect it. Ask yourself, *What would Future, confident Me do?*

You may need to take some of these steps before you feel you're 'ready' (remember, this is one of the non-negotiable success beliefs I shared in Chapter 1). This doesn't mean you have to leap right off the cliff; your comfort zone is elastic. You can stretch it a bit, then a bit more. Slow, steady, incremental progress will build your confidence and encourage you to continue. As you watch your efforts pay off, you'll think, *I am someone who can make progress and achieve things, whatever the external circumstances*. This thought is a great motivational boost, because when you anticipate success, you set yourself up to achieve. And when you achieve it, you begin to anticipate more. Plus, when you're having one of those down-on-yourself days, your incremental successes remind you to put things in perspective. Activities 25 through to 28 are key to building your confidence action plan, as well as a strong, confident core.

As you progress through your plan, remember that setbacks happen. They are unpleasant, but they don't have to be the end of the world because you get to choose how to respond to them. You can choose to think, *This is a catastrophe* or, *I'm a failure*. You can also choose to think, *This isn't great, but I'll overcome and learn from it*. I know the second thought can be challenging when we're in the middle of what feels like a disaster or a disappointment. So it's OK to retreat and lick your wounds for a while if you need to, as long as you learn from what didn't work and try again.

> ### 💡 ACTIVITY 25: Your strengths and successes
>
> Each time we meet, I ask my clients to share their progress, insights and thought shifts in a couple of sentences. This practice focuses on improvements, wins and successes, strengthening their confidence

muscles, re-wiring their neural pathways and giving them perspective. It's important because my clients are so often worried about what they've *not* done. (One of my clients calls this activity 'The reasons-I'm-not-s**t list'.)

Think about your last two or three years at work and in life. Write down all of the successes, achievements and accolades you can think of (not all of them will be work-related). What are you proud of? Why? What was your impact? If you were applying for a new job, what would you want to highlight? Be sure to recognise where you've made progress and overcome challenges and adversity and use strong, active verbs, such as 'champion', 'transform', 'spearhead', 'negotiate' and 'deliver'.

Take your time building this list and come back to it regularly. Add new successes as you achieve them. If you're planning to hunt for a new job soon, it would be wise to start this immediately.

💡 ACTIVITY 26: Take it to the team

One good way to grow and build your own confidence is to use your new knowledge to help others build and grow theirs. Try starting team meetings by asking the team to share their progress, achievements and insights, as well how they've overcome challenges. Recognising your team members' wins activates the feel-good hormone oxytocin, contributing to psychological safety and encouraging confidence. Discussing how team members approach and tackle difficulties demonstrates courage, tenacity, innovation and creativity.

💡 ACTIVITY 27: Area of focus

Take some space time to choose which area of your life your confidence action plan will focus on. Think about the aspects of your path to Future You where you lack confidence. Which of these low-confidence areas has the most impact on your goals? Does any area cause you more anxiety than the others? These questions will help you determine the best thing to focus on first.

As Step 1 of your confidence action plan, keep a log of these elements:

- **Goal:** Set your specific goal, using strong, active verbs about what you want to achieve, rather than what you *don't* want. Be specific. *I want to be more confident* is too vague and overwhelming to be useful. *I want to build my confidence presenting at team meetings so I can champion the decisions I think are best* is clear, actionable and purposeful.

- **Future You thoughts:** Write down how Future You carries themselves in this area. How do they behave, prepare or respond to adversity? Choose specific thoughts and actions. Write in the present tense.

- **Feelings:** Be sure to record your feelings through this process. How does your plan make you feel? How do you feel before and after taking actions? This will help you track your progress and manage your feelings.

- **Actions:** As you proceed, focus on improving one action at a time. Each morning, ask yourself, 'As I anticipate success, how will I embody confidence today?' As you improve, you will add new actions to the list and cross off the actions you complete.

📑 CASE STUDY 15: Sam

Sam's main coaching goal was to build her confidence and impact in her new role as an executive director. She waffled in executive team meetings (she said) rather than succinctly communicating her points. She felt flustered and more like a little girl than a senior leader. We talked through her goals and aspirations and chose an area of focus for her to improve her confidence. This is what her plan looked like:

Goal: I want to look and feel leaderlike and get my key points across clearly, succinctly and unambiguously.

Future Sam thoughts: I will read draft reports in advance of meetings and plan some statements or questions to show I'm on top of my brief. I will rehearse these out loud to practise speaking clearly and concisely. I will also run some of my ideas by a couple of key individuals before the meeting.

Feelings: These thoughts make me feel more grounded.

Actions: I will prepare myself mentally before the board meeting by visualising a successful meeting. I picture myself arriving at the board meeting a few minutes early with my papers organised. I walk calmly into the boardroom and take my seat. As others arrive, I acknowledge them with a nod or smile.

When the meeting begins, I tell the chair a few important things about the first agenda item. I know that the advantage of speaking up early is that I am more likely to do it again. As the meeting proceeds, I speak calmly and slowly, looking at everybody as I ask questions and make statements. When it's appropriate, I invite any comments or questions.

I also have a plan in case I am interrupted, which has happened frequently, up to now. I say, 'I would like to finish what I'm saying, please, and then I'd love to hear your ideas.' I say it slowly and assertively.

As Sam shared her log with me, she grew a couple of inches taller. Future Sam was in the room.

💡 ACTIVITY 28: Channelling alter egos

If you want to feel confident, prepared and grounded before a meeting, channelling an alter ego can help (one of the reasons I dislike back-to-back meetings is that they don't allow time for this). Your alter ego can be as simple or complicated as you please. My own alter ego is my inner Amazon. She's fearless, focused and energised. When I channel her, I'm taller, bolder and more resilient. I feel I can conquer the world.

The inner Amazon

For years, Beyoncé's alter ego, Sasha Fierce, helped her show up powerfully on stage. During a recent Claim Your Leadership Confidence challenge week I ran, attendees had a range of alter egos, including Piglet, David Beckham, Pink, a lion and Joan Collins' character from the 1980s soap opera *Dynasty*, Alexis Colby.

💡 **ACTIVITY 29: Seek out confident role models**

Look for someone in your life who has the type of confidence you wish to achieve. When you are with this person, pay attention to the way that they behave, carry themselves and respond to challenges. How does their confidence show up? Ask them for advice about cultivating and maintaining confidence, and consider how you might adapt their techniques to suit your style.

In this chapter, we discussed types of confidence and dispelled myths about it. You chose an aspect of your leadership life where you want to build your confidence and devise a plan to improve it. You now know how to build your confidence every day. We'll further explore confidence and influence in Chapters 11 through to 13. First, your key takeaways.

Key takeaways

- Action leads to confidence, not the other way around. Confidence comes from setting clear confidence goals, anticipating success and being open to learning from others. When you experience self-doubt, you know there's a way to work through it to the 'other side'.

- Confidence is different from self-esteem, arrogance and competence. Self-esteem refers to the way we see, accept and love ourselves. Arrogance refers to a sense of superiority over others and is often a defence mechanism that covers a lack of self-esteem. Competence refers to skill level, and works hand-in-hand with confidence. Leaders need both competence and confidence to shine.

- Choose an alter ego to help you on the path to confidence and ask yourself, 'What would this person do right now if they were in my shoes?'

- A confident leader hires great people and helps them to shine. Confidence and abundance are connected.

Creating your confidence action plan means choosing one specific area where being more confident will help you connect with Future You. Remember to keep notes of your achievements and successes as well as times when you overcame adversity. Doing this every day strengthens that belief muscle, builds new neural pathways and keeps anticipating success front of mind. A great daily confidence question? *'What would Future You want Current You to do right now?'*

11
Leadership Presence

We might use several expressions when describing how we want to be seen by others: executive presence, positive personal impact, gravitas. Whatever we call it, anyone can have it, no matter who they are or where they start. You can achieve leadership presence authentically without pretending to be someone you're not.

I have two colleagues who have a huge positive impact. When I'm with them, I feel energised, like a better version of myself. These two colleagues couldn't be more different. They have entirely different roles and backgrounds. One is male and extraverted. He is hugely knowledgeable and energetic, like a loveable Tigger. He is a master at helping leaders craft compelling stories. The other is an introverted female with a senior leadership position in the pharmaceutical industry. She has a quiet, thoughtful, calming presence, and her superpower is her ability to influence a wide range of characters, some of whom have big titles and bigger egos. What do these two people have in common? They are both warm, competent, credible, humble and able to connect with others regardless of background. They are willing to ask for help and admit they do not know the answer. They ask lots of questions and listen to the answers. Most important, when they are with you, they are 100% present.

You've probably been around people who were not fully present – with you in person, but their minds are elsewhere. They might be typing, scrolling or mentally writing their to-do list, but they're not actively listening to you. They might be looking over your shoulder to see if there is someone more interesting to speak to. That's the *opposite* of presence. When you have presence, you engage wholeheartedly and attentively with whoever and whatever you are doing without being distracted by external factors.

Despite best intentions, many leaders, teams and organisations lack presence. I suspect this is because they do not prioritise it. No organisation I know lists 'being present' on its competency frameworks. All too often, the norm is to run around like headless chickens because of the perception that sitting quietly and connecting 'takes too long' and 'everyone's too busy'. In this chapter, you will see how you can grow your leadership presence and why it's such a key skill at all levels of leadership. Activities 30 and 31 will help.

🔆 ACTIVITY 30: Set your presence intention

Ultimately, whether you have impact, presence and gravitas is less about you and more about how others feel when they're with you. Learning to listen deeply is a good starting point, and we'll discuss that in Chapter 12, but the most important thing is to focus your attention on the people you are with and the task at hand.

Decide to be fully present in your next meeting or one-on-one conversation. Anticipating success, set your intention right now: *I am someone who listens well.* Slow down, using your pause button. Use that time to digest and hear what someone is saying to you before rushing to respond. Afterwards, reflect on what you noticed. What did you discover? What felt difficult? What was different?

Imagine if everyone felt heard and valued in your presence. What impact would that have on the work and the people you work with?

🔆 ACTIVITY 31: How do you want people around you to feel?

Think about someone you know who has a positive leadership presence, such as a colleague, boss, peer or team member. How do they make you feel when you're with them? What behaviours make you feel that way?

Next, take a moment to consider how you want to make others feel in your presence. Write down the words or phrases that come to mind. Then, consider what you need to do or focus on to make that happen. For example, what might you need to pay attention to if your intention is to make people feel valued, motivated, engaged and comfortable speaking up? Or you want them to feel confident or creative? Future You's leadership presence comes from asking everybody what they need to show up as the best version of themselves. Imagine all the Future Yous that question could create.

📑 CASE STUDY 16: Caroline

My client Caroline told me she was always distracted, though I already suspected that, as Teams notifications kept pinging throughout our session. She felt like a butterfly, she said, flitting between email, WhatsApp and Teams messages without giving anyone or anything her full attention. You know by now that thoughts like *I'm always distracted* become self-fulfilling prophecies.

The impact of Caroline's distractedness was that she fired emails to her team that didn't make much sense, rather than thinking through her messages before sending them. Her meetings were long, poorly planned and lacked an outcome-focused agenda. Not only was she not performing at her best, but her team wasn't, either. These talented people were not the best versions of themselves around Caroline, and she knew that things had to change. Once she understood this, she set her intention: *I am someone who can focus and pay attention.* Anticipating success, our work began.

Cultivating warmth and competence

Research suggests that people use two universal, fundamental judgements to form opinions about others: warmth and competence. Warmth and connection are associated with trustworthiness, interpersonal skills, approachability and care for people's well-being. Competence is associated with ability, effectiveness, decisiveness and status (see Chapter 10, 'Confidence vs. competence'). As researcher Amy JC Cuddy explains in the *Harvard Business Review*, 'when we feel confident and calm, we project authenticity and warmth'.[17] Depending on the culture, organisation and social context, either warmth or competence may be more valued than the other, but whatever the context, authentically demonstrating both will undoubtedly improve your impact.

To borrow a term from author Mary Beth O'Neill, leaders need both 'backbone and heart' to cultivate leadership presence. O'Neill perfectly sums up leaders with impact as being 'compassionate

---

17 Cuddy, AJC, 'Connect, then lead', *Harvard Business Review* (1 July 2013), https://store.hbr.org/product/connect-then-lead/ r1307c?sku=R1307C-PDF-ENG, accessed 23 August 2024

with people, tough on issues'.[18] You may know leaders who are lovely, warm and bubbly but a bit wishy-washy. Like a loveable but daft labrador, these leaders are not as decisive or motivating as they might be. You may know highly intelligent, competent leaders for whom getting things done is more important than building relationships. This sort of 'cold fish' leader doesn't know how to read a room. They might make a big announcement about organisational change, then bang on about cost-saving benefits while everybody listening is worried they'll lose their job. As you can see, leaders with only one of these qualities do not have the kind of presence Future You will need. You must develop both warmth and competence.

Caroline Goyder sums this work up perfectly in her book *Gravitas*. Leadership presence, which Goyder refers to as 'gravitas', requires that '[you] chip away at what you don't need (the old anxieties, bad habits of speech and body language, negative beliefs about yourself) until you get to the heart of who you are.'[19] You'll probably notice that this description somewhat resembles the path we've carved out to get to Future You. Developing presence means banishing habits that no longer serve us and replacing them with new habits that are authentic and purposeful. This is

---

18 O'Neill, MB, *Executive Coaching with Backbone and Heart: A systems approach to engaging leaders with their challenges* (Jossey-Bass, 2011)

19 Goyder, C, *Gravitas: Communicate with confidence, influence and authority* (Vermilion 2015)

great news because it means you already know you can get there, whatever your starting point. You don't have to pretend to be someone else and you can use the lessons from this book to chip away at unhelpful thoughts and beliefs. Activity 32 will help you get there.

💡 ACTIVITY 32: What's the difference?

Think about a time when you demonstrated leadership presence and felt connected to the best version of yourself. Describe that time in as much detail as possible, evoking all your senses:

- What happened just before the event?
- What were your thoughts before and during the event?
- Think about your body. Were you sitting, standing or moving around?
- What were you feeling? Be as specific as possible.
- What did you hear and see around you?
- What made you feel good about the event. Name specific elements that made you feel good.
- What did you say, and how did you say it?
- What was the outcome or result of the event?
- What did you do after the event?
- What worked well enough that you would do it again? What didn't work?

Next, repeat the activity, recalling a time when you *didn't* have a strong leadership presence. Work through the same questions as above.

Finally, compare the two experiences to each other. What did you do differently that impacted your leadership presence? How did your feelings and physiology affect your performance? What will Future You do differently next time?

Thinking about times when you successfully and unsuccessfully demonstrated the presence you wish to cultivate will help you to learn from the experience and improve your presence. Once you know what helped you and what didn't, you'll be able to get there faster in the future. If you're unsure about the presence you have, I recommend asking three or four people you trust to share specific examples of when they've seen you at your best and most effective. That will give you many clues about how you come across to others.

📑 CASE STUDY 17: Julia

Julia came to me disappointed that a task she thought she'd articulated clearly to her team had not been completed. Though it didn't feel like it initially, the incident was helpful because it highlighted some of Julia's blind spots. When we discussed what was missing from Julia's presence and performance, she recognised a pattern.

She told me she was always rushing to 'just do this thing' before her meetings, which stopped her from being grounded or present. She did not believe she could slow down at first: 'I'll never be able to pause for seven seconds,' she told me, then paused for twelve when we practised. She also found her questions to her team didn't dig deep enough because she backed off when worried about upsetting them. That hot thought, 'I might upset them' got in her way.

Julia listed five things that Future Julia would do differently:

1. Clearly state her intent, desired outcomes and expectations for future discussions.

2. Double-check that people understand what she's asked them to do by summarising it back to her in their own words.

3. Increase transparency on deadlines and next steps, explicitly stating expectations and deadlines. For example, 'When we meet on Friday, I'd like you to give me a clear status update for project X and confirm which actions have been completed.'

4. Trust what she describes as her 'inner wise owl', following her intuition and asking questions when she suspects her team isn't progressing, even when they tell her they're 'on it'.

5. Slow down and give people time to answer questions.

Once she'd drawn up this list, she was able to practise these skills daily, which meant she improved her leadership presence and her confidence. This meant the speed and quality of her team's work improved, too.

🔍 CASE STUDY 18: The team comedian

I once worked with a wonderful and talented woman known as the 'team comedian'. Growing up, she'd received lots of rewards and praise for making her family laugh, and she continued to play the joker at work. Her big goal was to get a promotion, but she'd been unsuccessful. While she was warm and talented, nobody could imagine her in a more senior role. Her organisation was a traditional, heavily regulated organisation where seriousness and gravitas were considered essential. Her colleagues and bosses didn't see her as serious, authoritative or competent at a senior level.

My client knew the result she wanted: a promotion. To achieve this, she needed to grow her authority without having, as she called it, a 'personality bypass'. She started paying attention to her thoughts, noticing the ones that made her uncomfortable. This helped her recognise a pattern of behaviour that had played out from early childhood: her default position was to inject humour into a situation when she felt uncomfortable. She realised she did this to feel safe and believed it helped others feel safe, too. Sometimes her humour lightened the mood, but other times, it was a mechanism to deflect serious or difficult issues. Her colleagues saw through this and this diminished her leadership presence.

With this knowledge, she learned to sit with her discomfort rather than jumping in to 'rescue' with a joke. She no longer feels she must make everybody laugh, and she didn't need a personality bypass to change all of this. She just needed to improve her presence by cutting out the behaviours that diminished her perceived competence. She got that promotion eventually – in a competitor organisation.

Verbal and nonverbal communication

You may be familiar with Albert Mehrabian and Susan R. Ferris's 7-38-55 rule, which states that only 7% of all communication is done through words, whereas the nonverbal components comprise the rest: 38% of communication occurs through vocal tone and 55% through body language.[20] Research suggests that where our verbal and nonverbal communication is incongruent, we are more likely to take our message from nonverbal communication. Though words can be scripted, nonverbal cues are seen as spontaneous, genuine indicators of our feelings or intentions. Think how often you've seen someone read a script they don't believe in. The more they try to appear sincere and authentic, the more we see through them. We sometimes call this the 'authenticity doom loop' (politicians, take note).

Despite its usefulness, Mehrabian and Ferris's research is often misunderstood, misapplied and oversimplified. Communication is complex, dependent on both

---

20 Mehrabian, A, and Ferris, SA, 'Inference of attitudes from nonverbal communication in two channels', *Journal of Consulting Psychology*, 31/3 (1967), 248–252, https://psycnet.apa.org/record/1967-10403-001, accessed 23 August 2024

context and culture. It's also true that to some extent, we hear and see what we choose to, experiencing everything through our own filters and biases. Being aware of these will highlight the assumptions we might be (wrongly!) making and reduce their negative impacts.

Body language

How do you 'own' the room – displaying warmth and competence?

Body language can unintentionally lead to assumptions about ability, personality or approachability. If someone appears uncomfortable in a situation, people may assume they're nervous and not in control. Having arms folded for warmth could be mistaken for being closed or hostile. Changing your body language can also make you feel different. If you want to 'own' a room, it starts with your body language.

Let's think about posture, for example. We're often unaware of our posture (which is dangerous for our musculoskeletal health, if nothing else). I sat up straight as I wrote this – maybe you just did, too. Imagine there's an imaginary string pulling the top of your head toward the ceiling. Pull your shoulders back and plant your feet firmly on the floor. How do you feel now? How do you feel when you slouch and slump? I feel like I own my space when I stand straight. I feel more confident, powerful and alert–less constricted. My voice carries further. Good posture brings out my inner Amazon.

Body language is equally important in digital spaces, such as video calls or remote meetings. I once met a new client on Zoom whose camera revealed only the top of her head. I asked her to shift her camera angle. Once I could see more of her, she had a more powerful presence. Sometimes, even tiny tweaks make a significant difference.

Another simple way to improve your presence is to be purposeful with your movement. Stillness can be powerful. Think about anyone you know who can command the room without saying much. The late Queen Elizabeth II is a great example. There's no fidgeting, hair flicking or toe tapping to distract us from the message. They might not say much, but every word counts. One thing I can guarantee. They've mastered their breathing.

💡 **ACTIVITY 33: Walk into that room as if...**

There's something very powerful about mindfully 'showing up' physically as the leader you want to become. Every day. This means paying attention to how you walk into the room or virtual room. How you hold yourself. How you 'own' the space. How you acknowledge or welcome people. Does Future You rush in apologetically and make yourself look small or does Future You walk in slowly and calmly, head held high? To help you with this, you might imagine how someone you admire might walk into the room. You can also imagine how you would address each individual in the room. Channel Future You physically before every meeting, presentation or conversation, and notice what shifts for you (and how others respond to you).

The Symphony of Voice and breath

Our voices convey energy and emotion. Our pitch, pace, volume and intonation all influence how impactful we are. How do we convey passion or urgency? How do we give a 'difficult' message with care and compassion? How do we get a new idea across so people understand it easily? How do we keep people engaged? How do we make our message compelling or more relatable? How do we project our voice to command attention? When we speak with genuine emotion, from passion or anger or hope, for example, people sit up and pay attention. It can be an effective way to connect with your audience because it shows that you are invested and empathetic, and you care deeply about the subject. We can learn a lot from what actors do to prepare for a performance. Activity 34 will help you to better express emotion with your voice.

Intonation is the rise and fall of vocal pitch. It can give our speech dynamism and energy and make it more compelling. My own voice is naturally flat, so I consciously try to intonate more, particularly when speaking to large groups. Years ago, I asked someone to help me improve my presentation skills. She encouraged me to exaggerate my intonation to increase its range; she called the intonation range the 'top, middle and bottom of the stairs' voices. I felt self-conscious while trying it, but what felt exaggerated to me sounded natural when I watched the recordings later.

I often work with talented leaders who tell me they struggle to engage people. 'I know I speak too fast,' they often tell me, 'especially when I'm nervous.' When we say a lot in one long, unstructured monologue, our listeners can't keep up. They may miss much of what we say, or get frustrated and zone out. 'Hellomynameislynnscottnicetomeetyou', is much trickier to understand than 'Hello. My name is Lynn Scott. Nice to meet you', but the words are exactly the same. The only difference is the pauses. Pauses are powerful. You know that already if you've been using your metaphorical pause button. Paying attention to your breathing will help you to relax and slow down.

Of all the things we can do to improve our mood, comfort level and well-being, breathing may be the most important. They way we breathe can affect our stress and focus levels, physiological state, physical and mental performance, and voice. Most of us don't breathe properly, leading to dry throats, hoarseness and easily running out of breath. To get better, practise diaphragm breathing (abdominal or belly breathing). I'm a big fan of Dr Andrew Weil's 4-7-8 breathing technique,[21] but you can research many other options. Once you find a technique you like, practise using it during times of high stress or nervousness or when you're having trouble regulating your emotions. This will improve your posture, body language, voice and speech delivery and ultimately your presence.

⚡ ACTIVITY 34: Prepare your voice

How do we convey passion or urgency when we speak to an audience? How do we give a 'difficult' message with care and compassion? When your voice is expressive, dynamic and properly prepared, you will be better prepared to get new ideas across without confusion and keep people engaged. Your message will be more compelling and relatable. Actors are a great source of information on vocal expression. They are experts at breathing well, projecting their voice and employing a wide range of intonations that express energy and emotion. Here are some tips that actors use to prepare for a performance:

21 Weil, A, '4-7-8 breathing: Health benefits and demonstration', Andrew Weil, MD, 2024, www.drweil.com/videos-features/videos/the-4-7-8-breath-health-benefits-demonstration, accessed 23 August 2024

- Try speaking 'in character' (in the voice of another person). You can choose any type of person you'd like: a politician, chat show host, DJ, Winnie the Pooh or Hermione from Harry Potter. Deliver your speech or presentation as if you were that person. This will get you in the habit of paying attention to your voice and adjusting it to suit your purpose.

- You can also do a vocal warm-up, which both actors and singers do before they perform. Sing a few scales (do, re, mi fa, sol, la, ti, do) to prepare your voice. Say the letters of the alphabet out loud using a variety of pitches, speeds and volumes. You'll want to go from one extreme to another, from high pitch to low, slow to fast, quiet to loud.

- Drink water before you speak to hydrate your vocal chords. This will keep your voice from cracking and your throat from drying out.

☀ ACTIVITY 35: Experimental speaking

Find a text that contains about 150 words and record yourself saying it. Record it several times, experimenting with your pace, volume and intonation as you read it. The first time you record, say the text as you normally would so that you can compare the difference.

During subsequent recordings, experiment with different ways of showing warmth, credibility and competence. Emphasise different keywords or phrases. Find out how your voice changes when you sit down or stand up.

Tip: Try slowing down and pausing when you make an important point. Speed up where you want to inspire energy and enthusiasm.

As you practise this, you'll quickly learn how to speak to maximise your impact.

Verbal communication

As with body language and voice, verbal communication is more impactful when we do it with purpose.

We've all listened to people who never use one word when three will do. When these people drone on and on, we simply stop listening. Short sentences are easier for listeners to follow and give speakers a chance to breathe properly. Don't let your words get lost in a huge word salad. This applies to both the spoken and written word; there's a reason we love a concise 'plan on a page' rather than a verbose long-winded report. This morning, for example, I've been looking at a client's CV. It initially read, 'I am fully experienced in providing concise and insightful communications to various stakeholders', which is clear enough, but verbose. We changed it to 'I provide straightforward and insightful communications to my stakeholders' – it's punchier and clearer and we've lost the unnecessary filler words.

Consider the advertising slogan. Slogans are often short, but they're also near-universally understood and memorable even to children – they're so memorable that we remember them for decades:

- Keep calm and carry on.

- Should've gone to Specsavers.

- Just do it.

- It's finger-lickin' good.

All these messages are simple to remember and repeat. When you're speaking, particularly in front of large groups, it might help to prepare your words with a snappy slogan in mind to keep you on track.

Improving your leadership presence requires close attention to the way you carry yourself, the words you use, the energy in your voice and the actions you take. Strong leadership presence is intentional and efficient, projecting calm, warmth and competence – and now you know how to achieve it. With more presence and confidence comes a stronger ability to influence. In Chapter 12, we will work on improving your influence even further. First, your key takeaways.

Key takeaways

- People with leadership presence have credibility, humility, warmth and competence. They can connect with a wide variety of people because they ask for help and advice when they need it, show curiosity, listen and focus on the people they are with. They're comfortable with who they are and they inspire confidence in others.

- Your body language, energy, voice tone, pace and intonation and the words you use all impact your impact. How does Future You show up in the room?

- Breathe well.

- Learning to be concise and crystal-clear will elevate your leadership presence. Never use three words where one will do.

- Stillness and silence can convey leadership presence. There is no need to constantly 'fill the space'.

12
Track Your Influence

Influence is the power to change or affect someone or something which of course is a big part of leadership. If you demonstrate warm and competent leadership presence, you've got a head start. In this chapter, we'll examine common barriers to influence and I'll introduce you to my three legs of influence and help you to balance them.

Influence is sometimes confused with manipulation, but the difference between the two is crucial: *intent*. Influence is typically characterised by transparency, positive intent, integrity, authenticity and a desire to do the right thing for the greater good (although definitions of what that is may differ). When a leader has strong, positive influence, you're not forced or obligated to do something; you're motivated to do it, whether someone's watching or not. Manipulation, however, is associated with coercion, hidden motives, self-interest, exploitation, control, deceit and a disregard for the well-being of others. Manipulative leaders are not interested in the greater good. They are motivated by what's best for them and disinterested in the cost to others.

People can usually tell when their leaders have good intentions. They know when leaders care and want to do the right thing, even if they cannot articulate it well. 'He has a good heart', she might say, or, 'She cares'. If you're not sure whether you are being influential or manipulative, here's the litmus test: if your behaviour was reported in the Sunday press, would you be proud, or would you be embarrassed or ashamed? Let that be your guiding light.

Three barriers to leadership influence

Barrier 1: Lack of confidence

One significant barrier to strong influence is insecurity. As we've discussed, our thoughts, beliefs and the labels about ourselves affect our behaviour and, therefore, how others view us. For example, leaders without confidence often use diminishing, over-apologetic language that downplays their ideas, needs or experience (such as 'so sorry to ask, but...', 'I may be wrong, but...' or 'just off the top of my head...'). These phrases, full of diminishing language, are an influence killer. For a refresher on building leadership confidence, see Chapter 10.

Barrier 2: Lack of connection

Leaders who make every issue about them – their goals, their reputation, their bottom line – will not find influence easily. Suppose your CFO is fixated on shaving £2m off your expenditure this year. She won't do cartwheels of excitement when you ask her to sign off on a shiny new well-being package unless you can demonstrate how it will reduce absenteeism, sickness, recruitment costs and much more, thus contributing to that £2m saving.

If you talk vaguely about self-care, yoga, mindfulness and tree-hugging (OK, I'm exaggerating here), your CFO will likely say, 'Not bloody likely.'

The stereotypical example of the person who makes it all about them and their goals is the car salesperson who says, 'This car does a million miles to the gallon, and we've got a great finance deal', when you're far more interested in how safe it is for your children.

You're halfway there when you see people sit up and pay attention. You're speaking their language, speaking about something important to them and speaking about something they strongly agree or disagree with.

Barrier 3: Lack of listening

Good listening is a crucial influence strategy, but you can probably count on one hand the truly great listeners in your life. This is because deep listening is a skill many people have never learned or practised. We're so busy trying to get through the day, we 'half listen' and miss some key messages. Or people don't bother asking us because they know we're 'too busy' to give them our attention. Although it sounds counterintuitive, deep listening can save time in the long run. When we listen actively, we pay attention not only to what others say, but also their body language and facial expressions. We pay attention to the speaker's thoughts and feelings while managing our own. Active listeners listen with intention and clarity about their goals for the conversation. They check in frequently to ensure they maintain focus and understand what is being said.[22] This type of listening builds trust and confidence in leaders, increasing their influence.

---

22 Gallo, A, 'What is active listening?', *Harvard Business Review* (2 January 2024), https://hbr.org/2024/01/what-is-active-listening, accessed 23 August 2024

The three-legged stool of influence

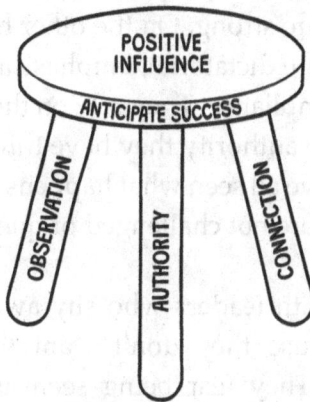

The stool of influence

Influence, like a sturdy stool, stands on three legs of equal importance. Like a stool, if one leg is shorter or weaker than the others, your influence will wobble. As you read the description of each leg, consider which one you'd like to strengthen first.

Leg 1: The authority leg

The authority leg holds your credibility, authority, reputation, knowledge, qualifications, experience, previous success and track record. It comes from everything you have done or achieved in your past.

Having authority or being *authoritative* is not the same as being *authoritarian*. When you are authoritative, you show that you know what you're talking about through knowledge and experience. This inspires trust and confidence, particularly when your other influence legs are strong. On the other hand, authoritarian leaders are dictatorial, emphasising command, control and compliance. They rely on their 'positional authority' – the authority they have through position or job title. We've all seen what happens when authoritarian leaders are not challenged or questioned.

I've worked with leaders who shy away from their authority because they don't want to be seen as authoritarian. They fear being seen as 'the critical parent' or 'the persecutor'. Or they fear not being liked. Their Future You work includes learning how to become more comfortable with that authority. They learn that you can be authoritative *and* caring – it's not an either/or. They learn that you can deliver clear, direct and sometimes tough messages with empathy and authority. Being comfortable with being authoritative is a big part of developing our leadership confidence and influence.

Leg 2: The connection leg

The connection leg holds your ability to connect, listen and build relationships and rapport with a wide range of people (not just 'people like us'). Your connection leg includes your empathy and compassion.

Building relationships and understanding what makes other people tick are key to influence. As the old saying goes, 'People don't care how much you know until they know how much you care'. Influential leaders make it a priority to get to know people on a human level. It will pay dividends in myriad ways for you and them. Before they buy into your vision, strategy or mission, people need to buy into *you*. When you invest time in building trust and strong relationships, things become easier, smoother and more collaborative. You can have a difficult conversation, agree to disagree, deliver and hear any constructive criticism without being threatened.

Spend time getting to know the human being behind the title. Start to understand their challenges, opportunities, and what keeps them up at night. Build sincere, genuine alliances because you'll need them–and so will they.

If you're frustrated with members of your team, how do you show empathy and compassion towards them when you're angry? This is when your pause button comes into its own. Empathy involves understanding and acknowledging on an intellectual level why your team member might be doing what they're doing, even if you don't agree with it. Emotional empathy means you understand and feel their pain as they navigate the challenge.

Compassionate empathy is more than that; it leads to actions aimed at supporting this team member specifically. It might mean saying, 'I can see how much there is on your plate. I've got some ideas to lighten your load if you're up for hearing them.' This type of invitation opens the door to a broader conversation without blaming or shaming your team member. You can feel all the empathy and compassion in the world, but if people don't hear it from you, they won't know. Showing empathy and compassion to a team member or indeed anyone you find 'tricky' is a key leadership skill. When you combine it with your authoritative voice, it's a true superpower we can all develop.

🔍 CASE STUDY 19: Katy

My client Katy was promoted to the head of a big legal team. She told me she was excited, but there was a lot to do. She was firing off emails right and left to ensure nobody dropped a ball. Katy believed she'd hit the ground running, but she had a blind spot. All this 'busy' work sat on shaky ground because Katy needed to strengthen her connection leg.

Her *intention* was good, but her *impact* was poor, and her team was fed up. Meetings were disorganised with no apparent purpose or agenda, and there was a constant barrage of orders with no clear direction of travel. When Katy received 360 feedback six months into her new role, it was tough for her to hear. Her team described her as dedicated but demanding and disorganised. At first, Katy was angry and tearful, but she eventually realised she needed to take a step back and get to know her team. She took time to understand their background, context and strengths. She also created space time for herself to think about her role rather than trying to be all things to all people.

Simply put, Katy had to slow down to speed up. This feels counterintuitive when the list of tasks and priorities is never-ending, but there's a time for getting stuff done and a time for slowing down and building relationships. Once Katy did the second, the first became easier.

Leg 3: The observation leg

The observation leg is probably the trickiest one to master. It holds the insights, hunches and details you pick up (spoken and unspoken) during a conversation or meeting to influence change. It comes from strong listening and through paying careful attention.

Leaders with a strong observation leg know how to bring up the elephant in the room honestly and sensitively. They know how to reframe a situation to bring out new ideas. They might sense the team are just going through the motions and probe to discover what's really on their minds or voice what everybody sees, but nobody is saying.

These leaders ask simple but powerful questions that illuminate groupthink and get people back on track. They make insightful observations without judgement: 'I notice we've talked a lot but not made any decisions – should we go there next?' These types of questions or observations may get a variety of reactions, from temporary discomfort to sighs of relief.

What they *always* do, however, is help people get unstuck, often from old patterns or ways of doing things, and move forward. Leaders with strong observation are great at both reading the room and knowing what to do with what they've read.

You can grow your influence effectively and with integrity by strengthening your skills of authority, connection and observation. Deep listening will help you build genuinely strong working relationships and collaborations and understand other people's worlds. In Chapter 13, we will conduct your influence audit and learn ways to further grow your influence. First, your key takeaways.

Key takeaways

- Manipulation and influence differ in intent. The intent of influence it to improve circumstances for everyone, while the intent of manipulation is to improve circumstances for yourself.

- The three main barriers to leadership influence are lack of confidence, connection and listening.

- The 'stool of influence' comprises three legs: authority, connection and observation. Each of these legs is equally important to your influence. Future You has a well-balanced stool.

13
Build Your Influence

Once you're familiar with the stool of influence, we can work on strengthening it. Many leaders favour one of the legs over the other two, leading to uneven, wobbly leadership. Well-rounded, influential leaders are able to use all three legs appropriately. Once you understand each of the legs, consider which would you like to work on first. The information and activities in this chapter will help you strengthen it.

Strengthening the authority leg

Does the thought of being 'authoritative' make you uncomfortable? Do you prefer a more democratic, reach-a-consensus-together style? Whilst this is to be celebrated most of the time, there are times when you have to say 'this is the way it is'. Of course, decision by committee can feel safe. You're all responsible if something goes wrong; safety in numbers and all that. But this is often why things move at a glacial pace; people think you don't listen, and they get fed up waiting for a decision. No one is doing the bold and courageous thing.

A leader with a weak authority leg might say, 'So sorry – I know you're really busy, but the exec is chasing me again. Would you mind starting work on those monthly figures? Let me know if that's OK.' That same leader's future self, on the other hand, might say, 'The monthly figures are due in two weeks, and I'd like you to start working on those as a priority. If you have any concerns about the deadline, please come to me today so we can find a way to make it happen. I have every confidence that you'll be able to do this.' Notice that the second request is clearer and more direct than the first, giving specific instructions while encouraging and showing respect for the team member.

I've found that women can be uncomfortable showcasing their achievements and expertise, preferring to talk about what 'the team' did. Of course, you want to recognise, value and reward the team. But *you* are the leader of said team.

So, own what you did and be proud of your achievements, strong leadership and track record. Use 'I' as well as 'we'. Sometimes, there is an 'I' in a team. And as one of my (male) clients said this week, 'Maybe men need to use 'we' more.'

Sadly, we've all heard stories of women in authority being described as 'bossy' or 'ball-breakers', or worse. Descriptions that are rarely given to a man in authority. There is still more work to be done on this, and we'll keep going.

One simple thing you can do to improve your authority is to practise using 'I' daily, as well as 'we'. Activity 36 will help you to trust your own authority. Activity 37 will help you to better express it.

💡 ACTIVITY 36: Notice your thoughts

By this point, you should have plenty of experience noticing your thoughts. To improve your authority, pay special attention to thoughts that prevent you from asserting your authority when a decision must be made or an instruction or feedback given.

Ask yourself what Future You would think in this situation. What advice would they give you? How would they feel about giving these instructions, sharing that feedback or announcing this decision? Imagine being in this situation as Future You, working to balance your authority with your compassion.

> ☀️ **ACTIVITY 37: Practise decisive language**
>
> Write down what you want to say in an authoritative voice. Pay attention to the difference between what you might normally say and what authoritative Future You says. Where do you normally use diminishing language or over-apologise? Delete those words!
>
> Once you've got a clear, compassionate and direct speech written, practise saying it out loud. You may feel uncomfortable, but remembering to breathe and channel authoritative Future You will help. Think about how Future You speaks and carries themselves. If you're struggling, you might look for some role models who are good at this. Observe what they do that demonstrates their authority. If it helps, you can borrow my inner Amazon.

Strengthening the connection leg

In my experience, too little time and space is given to this leg in busy organisations, where relationships can be transactional at best. When we're scoring points, working in silos, struggling with deadlines and fixated on being right, our ability to see other perspectives diminishes and we get tunnel vision. Sometimes seeing the world from the 'I' rather than the 'we' lens has value particularly when we're building our authority leg. But when you're looking to connect, it can reduce – and may even destroy – your ability to influence others. I suspect that we neglect this leg because we tell ourselves we're too busy ploughing through our 'to do' list and getting stuff done. Maybe you think connecting with people at a deeper level involves meaningless small talk or cringey icebreakers or team events. But remember this: sometimes small talk can make the big talk happen much more easily.

The first step to strengthening this leg is making time to do so. Spend time getting to know the humans behind the job titles. Work toward understanding their challenges, opportunities and stresses. Influence requires sincere, genuine alliances. Prioritise cultivating as many relationships of this type as possible. The more connected you are to key people, the more sounding boards you will have when you want to influence a decision. Even if others disagree with a decision or request, you've built enough trust and goodwill with them that you can have an honest discussion and work through it. A wide network of connections will also help you raise your profile across and outside of your organisation. Whether we like it or not, having strong relationships with others smooths many a path – remember there's a lot of truth in the saying, 'It's not what you know, it's who you know'.

Another method to improve connections is to look for ways to assist others in your organisation. When you do something positive for someone else, they are more likely to respond in kind. Social psychologist Robert

Cialdini discusses the concept of reciprocity in his book *Influence: The Psychology of Persuasion.*[23] His research and observations suggest that when people receive a favour, they feel a sense of obligation to reciprocate at some stage so this can generate huge amounts of cooperation and goodwill. Here are some sample conversation starters that have worked well for leaders looking to build their influence more widely:

- 'I liked what you said in our meeting about the roadmap. We used something similar to that in my last organisation, and I have some contacts and resources that might help you. Can we get together to go through them?'

- 'I've found some data that will help with your project. I'd love to get our heads together for thirty minutes so I can share it with you.'

- 'I have some ideas that would simplify the recruitment process for our engineers. Let me know if you'd like me to set up a half-hour meeting to discuss them.'

- When you've built up a relationship with someone and need to ask for a favour, try this: 'I'm working on building my strategic skills, and I've noticed you are good with strategy. I would value thirty minutes of your time for some guidance.'

---

23 Cialdini, RB, *Influence: The psychology of persuasion,* new and expanded edition (Harper Business, 2021)

The thing with reciprocity is it must be genuine and not manipulative – if you're insincerely exploiting reciprocity for personal gain people will see through you. And none of us likes to feel manipulated.

> ### 💡 ACTIVITY 38: Be the better person
>
> If you've had a brittle relationship with someone at work, this is your chance to show Future You leadership and change things. Anticipating success, invite them for coffee or a drink. Tell them, 'I know we've not always seen eye to eye, but I think we can change that and work better together. What do you think?' If they don't bite, move on. You're not responsible for other people's behaviour. If they accept, however, you've got a real shot to improve your influence – and your working life.
>
> Start by anticipating success. Practise deep listening. Remember they are human and are, most likely, trying to do a good job. Ask questions and listen to the answers without rushing in or interrupting. You can't change the past, but you can create a better working future together.

> ### 📑 CASE STUDY 20: Lars
>
> Lars, a newly promoted head of strategy development, couldn't understand why so much time was spent before each board meeting on so-called 'chit-chat', so

he didn't engage. As a result, others didn't know him and therefore didn't know whether to trust him. Not surprisingly, he found it hard to get people on board with his ideas.

Lars needed to improve his ability to connect on a human and emotional level, not just on a business or task level, so I set him some experiments. I had him ask people at the office about their lives outside work, building on their pre-meeting small talk. I also had him chat with strangers in shops.

Lars initially found this cringey, but he got over it. What felt like a chore at first became genuinely interesting after a while. He began to pride himself on listening. As people opened up to him, he shared more about himself, and he saw how small talk made big talk happen more quickly. His influence grew stronger at work. Better, he struck up a conversation with a woman he met on one of his business flights in the check-in queue and went on to marry her. If that's not a good reason to strengthen your connection leg, I don't know what is.

Strengthening the observation leg

If you want to strengthen your observation leg, the best way to is to slow down (see Chapter 2). Like the connection leg, the observation leg depends heavily on deep listening and paying close attention to people and process. Developing strong powers of observation means tuning your antennae to subtleties like what is *not* being said, the energy (or lack thereof) in the room and the body language and voices of others. Your focus should be on what is happening and its impact on the people around you. This skill takes time, dedication and careful attention to develop.

Fly on the wall

💡 ACTIVITY 39: Be a fly on the wall

Do this exercise when your required contribution and input are minimal so you can observe others closely. Work to be fully focused and present, dropping any filters or biases and being as neutral as possible. What do you pick up?

Afterward, consider these questions:

- Who in the room had influence, and why? Which 'legs' did you see in action?

- Who read the room and helped the group shift direction if necessary?
- Who used significant data or facts that compelled people to act?
- Who gave more detail than people need?
- Who told inspiring stories or anecdotes to illustrate a point?
- Who got their message across succinctly and calmly? Who got it across with passionate and inspiring energy?
- Who built on ideas and opened up conversations?
- Who criticised ideas or shut conversations down?
- Who shared thoughts as facts?

Once you've answered these questions, consider how you might use your observations to improve your own influence and impact. What underlying tensions, weaknesses or anxieties exist? What raised your curiosity? Practise this exercise as often as you can; the more you do it, the more natural this type of observation will become. As you practise, take care to maintain empathy, compassion and curiosity, not judgement.

Here's what Alison, Chris and Paul learned from this exercise:

- Alison: 'Keeping everyone in the room happy seemed more important than peering under stones and being honest about what wasn't working. Everyone in the room colluded with this. As a new director, I found this a bit shocking. It was as if they had too much empathy for each other and none for the customers.'

- Chris: 'Dan, who is new, stopped when Suzi was being shouted down and said, "Hey, can we just stop for a minute? Let's hear Suzi out." It was a bit embarrassing, but also an eye-opener. Meetings have been much better since then.'

- Paul: 'Anne creates a sense of confidence and certainty in what she says. She knows her stuff, is well prepared, and never gets ruffled. She speaks quite slowly and quietly, so we must listen hard, but she clearly listens to and understands our challenges. It's clever, and I've learned a lot from watching her.'

📖 CASE STUDY 21: Gill

When I started coaching Gill, she was aimless and frenetic. One of her aspirations was to slow down and reflect more. Work was not getting done to the standard she expected, and she felt she hadn't been leading her team sufficiently or giving them clear direction. She attended a monthly project meeting she described as 'always tense'. People were defensive and protective of their departments, and finger-pointing and blame were common.

Gill decided to interrupt her team's pattern of attack and defence. She told me, 'I took a big, deep breath and said, "Right, how about we all stop for a minute. How's everyone feeling right now?"'

Tumbleweed.

Gill remembered her pause button and resisted the temptation to speak until someone spoke up, followed by someone else. An honest and emotional conversation ensued about how frustrated the group were with their slow pace. That was the break that helped them step back, re-evaluate and reset.

Gill observed the tension in the room and decided to address it by asking a question and then pausing. As you can see, this skill is precious. It can save time, facilitate honest dialogue and break entrenched patterns. That's influence at its best.

🔆 ACTIVITY 40: Influence audit

Think about a recent time when you had influence. Use the acronym STAR to describe the Situation, Task, Action you took and the Result you achieved. Set a timer for two minutes and say this out loud, recording your answer.

Next, think about a time when your influence was not successful. Which leg of influence was missing or weak? Remember, this is about *your* behaviours, thoughts and actions, not other people's. If you could go back in time, what would you change? Again, use the STAR acronym. Give yourself two minutes to speak, recording your answer.

When you've finished recording, listen back to both of your answers, comparing and contrasting them. Based on your comparison, what behaviours of yours take you closer to Future You? Which do you need to adjust?

🔆 ACTIVITY 41: 'Yes, and...'

This activity, based on a technique used in improvisational theatre, is a good one to try in a meeting or other group activity. When someone raises an idea, respond with 'Yes, and...', rather than 'No', or 'Yes, but...'. The idea is to accept and build from everyone's ideas, rather than rejecting them. This activity will get you thinking broadly and widely about the people you want to influence and which messages will get them on-side.

For example, 'I love the idea of a quarterly offsite *and* I'll see if we can find some way of funding it', is more encouraging than 'I love the idea, *but* we don't have any money'. The person who suggested the idea will likely feel more comfortable sharing their next idea with you if you respond to it the first way. The first example builds on the art of the possible with an anticipate-success approach, while the second closes down communication with 'computer says no'.

ACTIVITY 42: Know your audience

Consider a project or task you want to move forward. Think about the outcome or decision you want at the end of the discussion. Be clear about why your proposal benefits the people you want to influence.

This is where it gets interesting: not everybody is likely to be influenced by the same thing. For that reason, influencing people relies on knowing them. Consider the key players and different personalities, and ask yourself:

- What will get people to ask for more information?
- For what reasons might people say no?
- Who is likely to say yes right away, and why?
- How will you get a 'yes' from the person who holds the purse strings?

Know your audience

- How will you get a 'yes' from the person who wants headlines, not details?
- How will you get a 'yes' from the frazzled manager whose team will implement the change?
- How will you get a 'yes' from the nit-picker?
- Who do you need to get to know better to influence them?

The best way to sound people out is to share your idea briefly with each of them individually before going into a big meeting and presenting it. Listen – I mean *really* listen – to their responses, objections and questions without defending, justifying or attacking. You'll avoid unexpected curveballs in the meeting because you'll be able to tweak your presentation for the best chance of success.

As you prepare, consider how your presentation appeals to:

- People who want facts, figures and evidence-based data
- People who want to feel an emotional connection
- People who want all the details
- People who want to know if it will make, save or cost money
- People who like you and believe in what you're doing
- People who want to look good or make their life easier
- People who often think they or the team are too busy

If you've built strong relationships, you'll have a good idea of the message that will most appeal to each of these people. This is because you've seen these people in action, listened to them and noticed what's important to them. You know what causes them stress and how they like to receive information.

If you're still struggling to get everyone on the same page, it's likely that your common purpose or priorities are unclear. Hit the pause button to work on the issue. You should also look for and challenge either/or thinking, empire-building and conflicts of interests. Get your observation leg working.

More tips for building influence

Balancing your influence stool is not the only way to improve your influence. I want to share some tips that will help you influence when you are presenting an idea or proposal.

- Outline your problem, challenge, idea or opportunity succinctly and crisply. Remember 'Bottom line up front'.

- Your opening words should make people sit up and pay attention.

- Rhetorical questions can be helpful. 'We all agree that the software package we're using is not fit for purpose, *don't we?*' Everyone will nod, which means you've already got a yes.

- Give the data/proof/hard facts to back up your suggestion. Big picture first, detail only if you need it. Present this in a dynamic way so it's easy to understand. Crisp visual images rather than reams of data.

- Build an emotional connection – why does this matter to the human beings in the room with you?

- Give the long-term potential benefit or return-on-investment of agreeing to your proposal.

- Give the cost last, if there is one, because you want people to see the value and benefits first. You don't want to hear 'that's too expensive' or 'we don't have the budget for that' before you've outlined the benefits.

With all the preparation in the world, you can be thrown off course if you feel derailed, attacked or shouted down. You've lost the argument if you attack or become defensive. Instead, this is a good time to channel Future You:

- Rather than telling yourself, *He is trying to derail me*, reframe your thought as, *He needs more information from me*.

- Answer any questions neutrally and honestly, treating every question as if it is sincere, rather than assuming it's an attack.

- Remember your pause button.

- Respond, don't react.

Even the best leaders sometimes miss the mark. What should you do if you've outlined your plan and then you get ....tumbleweed?

- Press the pause button. The worst thing you can do is fill the space and keep talking.

- The best thing you can do is ask a specific question. For example, 'Jess, you and I discussed the financial figures last week. Is there anything you would add?' Or, 'Let's take five, and I'll take questions when you return.'

- Press the pause button again. Based on the answers to your question, how can you recalibrate and get back on track?

Will you always get what you want if you follow these tips? Unlikely. They will almost certainly improve your record and build your influence overall, however. The more people respect, trust and like you, the more yeses you will get.

📑 **CASE STUDY 22: Chris**

My client Chris couldn't understand why no one would let his team rework some business processes that were no longer fit for purpose. It was a no-brainer to him, but the more he insisted, the more his boss resisted. His boss was worried that changing the processes would upset the influential people who designed the originals. Chris needed to find another influence lever to pull.

Building on his strong relationships, he sought out a couple of allies who saw the benefits of his proposal and spoke to some of the original designers. 'These business processes were a good start,' he told them. 'We have some new management information now, so it's time to upgrade them. Can my team get guidance from you if we need it?' His diplomatic approach worked.

In this chapter, we worked on building the legs of your stool of influence. We discussed additional ways to build your working relationships, which will improve your ability to understand and overcome problems more quickly and with less pain. In Chapter 14, we will turn our attention to improving communication. First, your key takeaways.

Key takeaways

- Strengthening authority requires that we use 'I' language in addition to 'we' language. Noticing your thoughts and using decisive, unambiguous language will also improve authority. Remember, being authoritative is not the same as being authoritarian.

- Improve your connection to others by practising deep listening. Ask questions and listen to the answers. Pay attention to language, body language and voice and demonstrate curiosity and compassionate empathy. Pauses are powerful.

- Strengthening your observation leg requires paying close attention to others. Deep listening also plays a role. Be a fly on the wall at first, neutrally watching and noticing without getting involved. Once you've done this a few times, you can start to share your observations with curiosity, not judgement.

- Your influence will grow the better you know the people you work with because you will be better able to respond to their concerns, disagreements, ambitions, hopes and stressors. As human beings, whatever their title, most people are trying to do the best job they can. Never lose sight of that.

14
TLC – Trust, Listening And Communication

I'd be a multimillionaire if I had a pound for every person who told me that communication is 'terrible' in their organisation.

'Communication is terrible' can mean different things to different people at different times. *That's part of the problem.* We can only solve something when we're clear on what we're trying to solve. Poor communication adds to our cognitive burden because we must probe to discover what it means. Great communication, on the other hand, avoids ambiguity, confusion and assumptions and saves time.

I remember falling into the assumption trap myself as a new coach. A client would say, 'I want you to challenge me', and I'd say, 'Yes, of course', but my understanding of 'challenge' might differ greatly from theirs. I eventually found an easy solution: 'On a scale of 1 to 10,' I asked, 'how challenging does this feel?' I'd follow up with, 'Do we need to go higher or lower?' When in doubt, ask. Always.

When you hear a vague phrase like 'We need to communicate better', or 'You're not a team player', or 'That report was great', try 'double-clicking' on it instead of trying to work out what you think it means. This term comes from Judith E. Glaser, a researcher who worked on conversation and mind mapping.[24] In this context, 'double-clicking' means delving deeper and asking for more information, much as we double-click a link in an article to find out more on the subject. One of my engineering clients describe it as 'digging below the surface to get to the gold' which I rather like, too!

Trust in conversations

In the best conversations, participants trust each other and feel trusted and psychologically safe. They also feel secure enough to raise concerns, to disagree and to share anxiety or discomfort. When we feel heard and valued and conversations feel productive, we produce oxytocin, a feel-good hormone often known as the 'love' or 'bonding' hormone. Oxytocin improves

---

24 Glaser, JE, '"double-clicking" my way to success', The Creating WE Institute, January 2011, https://conversationalintelligence.com/news-blogs/articles-blogs/doubleclicking-my-way-to-success, accessed 26 August 2024

our ability to communicate, work with and trust others by activating networks in our prefrontal cortex. This doesn't mean we should succumb to groupthink. It means we can effectively debate, challenge and work towards the best solution without resorting to points-scoring or arguing.

Where trust is absent and we don't believe the people around us have our back, we may be hypervigilant. We may start to attack, defend or close down. We may become passive-aggressive or look for ways to sabotage. Alternatively, we might find ourselves people-pleasing or agreeing publicly even though we don't agree privately. That's survival mode: fight, flight, freeze or appease.

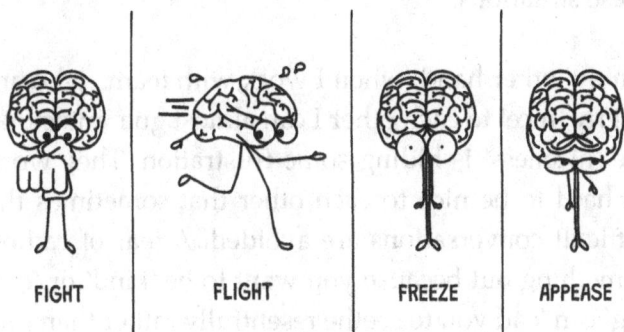

| FIGHT | FLIGHT | FREEZE | APPEASE |

Survival mode

When we lack mutual trust and feel threatened, we're constantly scanning our environment for danger, risk or threat. An eye-roll from our boss, tutting from a colleague, a pointed finger or a trigger word can send us into survival mode. Suddenly, we don't feel safe because of what that eye-roll means to us. (Those filters and biases, again.) Our body produces high cortisol and adrenaline levels when we feel fear, rejection, humiliation or criticism. All our energy is used to protect us from the 'threat', hindering our ability to think clearly and make rational decisions. The dreaded 'red mist' comes down, and we can't think straight, making us more likely to act on impulse. In these situations, the best thing you can do is use your pause button and/or walk away, taking some space time to focus on your breath and name what you're feeling (see Chapter 9). Other options include asking a question or saying, 'I would like to think about this before I decide.' Learning to respond not react is critical in these situations.

On the other hand, when I work with teams who are overly 'nice' to each other I can almost guarantee that the 'niceness' is hiding some frustration. They work so hard to be nice to each other that sometimes the difficult conversations are avoided. A fear of calling something out because you want to be 'kind' or 'caring' can lead you to seethe resentfully rather than risk rocking the boat. If this sounds familiar, it's time to work on some better Future You thoughts – because what are the consequences for you and others of biting your tongue and saying nothing?

Of course, it is possible to feel trust and distrust simultaneously. Uncertainty can have this effect, because it creates cognitive dissonance. Your brain is designed to seek patterns, make predictions and reduce ambiguity, so uncertainty makes it hard to know where you stand. That might make you anxious or uncomfortable, even if you're with people you generally trust. At times like these, I recommend keeping an open heart and mind until you have more data. This is easier when there is a baseline of mutual trust because we can discuss even sensitive or difficult topics and share different perspectives without coming to blows. Indeed, the way to get to calm, trusting waters is to navigate through the brambles and weeds of confusion and disagreement to get back on the right route. When you've got a strong observation leg (see Chapter 12) you can do this more easily.

Shut up and listen

If you asked 100 people to list the top ten traits of a great leader, I can almost guarantee that all 100 would include 'good listening' on the list. If you asked those 100 people whether they consider themselves good listeners, it's likely that most of them would say yes – or at least 'most of the time'. This likely doesn't align with your experience; it doesn't with mine. Some of these people might be deluded, but it's more likely that they aren't listening as well as they think and missing swathes of important information.

When we have a lot of plates spinning, it's easy to half-listen while we multitask, hoping to fix things quickly and move on. This doesn't work, however, because if we are not fully listening we don't completely understand the issue at hand, so can go off down the wrong track or make assumptions and waste lots of time. The following table includes some signs that you're not listening well enough and what you can do instead.

Hurdles to deep listening

Hurdle	What to do instead
Multitasking: Though most people believe they are good at multitasking, there's plenty of research to suggest that you really can't listen to me and write that email at the same time.	**Pay attention:** Give the person speaking your full attention. Write notes afterwards if you need to. If you're worried you'll miss something, ask them to summarise or email you their key points at the end of the conversation.
Rushing: When problems feel urgent, we may feel pressure to rush to a solution before we fully understand the problem.	**Pause:** Take some space time to think about the problem, or 'double-click' for more information. Be clear on the 'end in mind'.
Bias: We are all susceptible to interpreting what others say and making assumptions based on our filters and biases and our previous experiences of that person. If we do not recognise these biases, they can get in the way of clear communication.	**Recognise biases:** Pay attention to knee-jerk reactions that may illuminate your filters and biases. Notice your related thoughts. To ensure you've understood what the other person said, summarise back what you understood and double-click on anything ambiguous. Always assume positive intent.

Hurdle	What to do instead
Impatience: We can all experience irritation when we are talking to someone who goes on and on and on or habitually wanders off-topic. Losing our patience at these times, however, diminishes trust and open communication.	**Set limits:** Set yourself up for success by placing limits on meetings with people whose communication style irritates you. For example, tell the waffler you have five minutes to hear them out and structure the meeting using the 'Bottom line up front' method. If you don't need details, say so. Tell them you want the top three priorities or headlines or questions. Help them to help you.
Triggers: Sometimes, particularly where trust is thin or lacking, we feel personally attacked by someone else's comment and go into survival mode. We think they're trying to trip us up. But are they? Or are they, too, operating in survival mode?	**Regulate:** You can't listen well in survival mode. Use the emotional regulation strategies I shared in Chapter 9. Pause. Take time out. Did the person mean to attack? Are you sure? When in doubt the phrase 'say a bit more about that' will buy you breathing and thinking space.
Listening with an agenda: Sometimes when topics are fraught or there are disagreements, we fall into the trap of listening with a fixed view or to have our say. We may look for places where we can make our point and plan our rebuttal rather than listening.	**Listen to connect:** Rather than prioritising your own point, try prioritising your connection with the other person. How can you make them feel heard, understood and respected, even if you disagree? Why do they feel the way they do? Get clear on your joint 'end in mind' or desired outcome and work accordingly.

(Continued)

Hurdle	What to do instead
Interrupting: When we are excited about a topic, have strong ideas or opinions or feel anxious, we might interrupt more often. This both stops us from really hearing what others say, but also reduces their trust in us.	**Pause:** Before you speak, pause for five seconds. If you're not sure whether the other person is done, ask, 'Is there anything else you want to say?' before speaking. Sometimes you will need to interrupt because it's the right thing to do to keep everybody on topic. You can say, 'I'm going to stop you there for the time being so we can stay on track. I can come back to you later if there's more you want to say.'
Exhaustion: Our executive brains don't function well when we're tired, leading to poor communication.	**Rest:** If possible, take a power nap or relaxing break. Walk around or do some stretching. Know when your energy levels are at their highest and plan your day accordingly if you can.

If you have experienced deep conversations where all parties listen, you know how powerful it is, even if the conversation itself is not easy. Deep listening is an important and, sadly, rare skill. The best way to become a great listener is to set your intention to become one and to practise at every opportunity. The ideas in the table will help, as will the suggestions in Activity 43.

⌖ **ACTIVITY 43: Four listening activities**

If you want to build your listening skills, adding some or all of these four activities to your routine will help:

- Choose at least one conversation a day during which you mindfully practise your listening skills. Prioritise giving space, not interrupting and pausing. Pay attention to repeated words and play back metaphors.[25] Don't speak just to fill the silence; instead, say 'tell me more' to encourage the speaker to continue. The goal is to improve your listening by 1% each day.

- With permission, record a conversation with someone and listen back to it later. What did you pick up? What did you miss? Which of the hurdles to listening did you fail to clear? These questions will help you decide what you need to improve.

- Read up on listening. There's no shortage of great books that can guide you. I recommend Nancy Kline's book *Time to Think: Listening to Ignite the Human Mind* and her article 'The Ten Components', about how to establish a thinking environment.[26]

---

25 When you listen well, you'll notice the metaphors people use to describe themselves, others or situations. Those metaphors are powerful clues to how others are feeling, but don't try to interpret what you *think* they mean. Instead, double-click. If someone says, 'It feels like I'm going into battle', ask them to describe the battle. If they say, 'I need to get out of the weeds', ask which weeds they'd pull up first. These are some of the richest conversations you can have.

26 Kline, N, *Time to Think: Listening to ignite the human mind* (Cassell, 2002); Kline, N, 'The ten components', Time to Think, 2020, www.timetothink.com/thinking-environment/the-ten-components, accessed 26 August 2024

- Do a robust coach, counselling or similar training programme that includes practice, observation and real-time feedback from an experienced practitioner.

Being a good listener might feel frustrating initially, particularly when you're busy, but stick with it. It's one of the most brain-friendly, trust-building, time-saving Future You skills you can use.

🔍 CASE STUDY 23: Stuart

Stuart was frustrated and despondent. He thought he was giving clear instructions and guidance to his new team, but they weren't progressing fast enough in their three major projects. He asked me to observe a team meeting. When I did, I was surprised to find that he talked *at* his team for almost forty-five minutes of the hour. He threw in the odd 'Does that make sense?', but left no time for anyone to respond. His team looked like rabbits in the headlights.

He'd noticed the rabbit-in-the-headlights expressions (fortunately), but assumed they meant the team didn't understand what he was saying. Instead of pausing to ask a question, he gave them increasing detail 'to help them understand', going off on several tangents. At the end, with five minutes to spare, he said, 'Is that clear? Any questions?', but did not pause for answers. His team nodded and scuttled out of the room, clearly desperate to escape.

Stuart's a good guy – kind, hardworking and well intentioned. He is also a talker. Everything he thinks, he says out loud, stream-of-consciousness style. A big part of our work together was changing that pattern. When we discussed how the meeting went, he chose three things to do differently next time:

1. Ask everybody to attend the next meeting with a top-line update on their three key projects. They would have two minutes each to share and to tell Stuart what they needed from him to progress. He would dedicate the rest of the meeting to helping them make traction.

2. Remind everyone at the beginning of the next meeting of the meeting's purpose and leave time at the end for the team to recap. He would allocate fifteen minutes for all team members to summarise their subsequent actions and ask questions.

3. Ask questions that required more than a yes-or-no answer and use his metaphorical pause button.

We also chose some generic questions that he could ask if he got stuck or was tempted to talk *at* his team again:

- Can you tell me a bit more about that?
- Where are you stuck?
- What do you believe is the next step?
- Who else might you talk to for help with this?
- How can I support you with this?
- What are we not seeing?
- What's the bravest/quickest/easiest thing we can do now?
- What will you do first?
- And what else?
- What would Future You want to do?

- If you anticipate success, what will you do right now?

These questions are easy to remember and applicable in many different situations. Though Stuart's next meeting wasn't perfect, it was much improved over the first one.

Intention and impact

Intentions are invisible. It is often the case that our personal feelings about someone can colour our perception of what they say. We're more likely to assume bad intentions on the part of people we dislike, distrust or don't know well. It's important to notice our thoughts about others and resist negative assumptions based on personal feelings and past experiences. A good rule of thumb is to assume that others' intention is positive until we have evidence to the contrary.

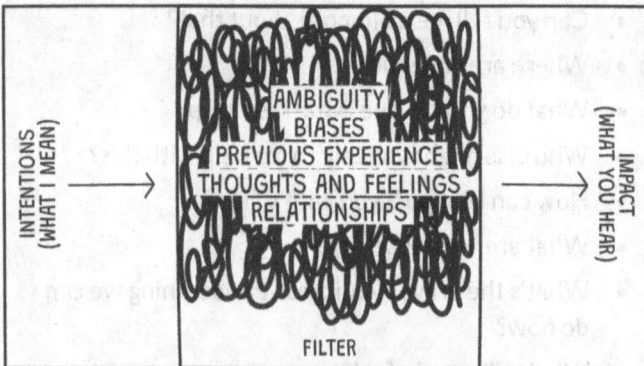

INTENTIONS (WHAT I MEAN)

AMBIGUITY
BIASES
PREVIOUS EXPERIENCE
THOUGHTS AND FEELINGS
RELATIONSHIPS

FILTER

IMPACT (WHAT YOU HEAR)

Impact and intention

It's also important to note, however, that positive intention doesn't always lead to positive outcomes. For example, maybe you have a team member who gives you reams and reams of detail every time she speaks. Her *positive intention* is to ensure you have the information you need, but the impact is that you spend thirty minutes gritting your teeth while she gives you lots of irrelevant information. Instead, help her have the impact she needs by telling her specifically what you *do* want. Rather than 'I don't need all the detail' tell her specifically what you do need to hear. Make it easy for both of you.

Maybe you have an angry team member who seems negative about everything, wants things to be 'right' for the customers and continuously moans about senior management. His *positive intention* is to stand up for customers. His anger comes from a strong belief about what is right. To improve his impact, you might try steering his energy toward taking positive action to improve the customer experience directly, focusing on what he can do, rather than what he can't.

Poor communicators may seem aggressive, abrupt, unhelpful or uncommunicative. It's easy to think of poor or problematic communicators as energy vampires, mood hoovers or troublemakers. The overwhelming likelihood, however, is that these people have positive intentions but feel threatened, uncertain or apprehensive and are trying to protect themselves and what they believe to be right in the only way they know how. You're halfway there if you can get behind their good intentions and steer them toward productive action. That doesn't mean you excuse behaviour that crosses a line, but make sure the line is clear. Be explicit about your expectations, boundaries and standards.

🔍 CASE STUDY 24: Richard

Richard complained to me that his boss, Anna, cancelled their one-on-one meeting 'yet again'. 'That's the second time this month,' he said. 'She doesn't care about people. It makes me feel like I'm not important.'

Later, he found out that Anna had been tasked with a highly confidential project, to which she had to give her all, reducing her availability for regular one-on-ones with Richard. Her *positive intention* was to maintain confidentiality at all costs, but the impact was that she repeatedly cancelled on Richard without explanation which made him feel undervalued.

In the absence of facts, our brains will make them up. If Anna had given Richard an explanation, he would have felt more valued. If Richard had assumed good intentions, he would have felt less angry.

If you think communication is poor, you can start by avoiding assumptions, recognising your biases and filters and assuming that most people have positive intent. Deep listening, double clicking, being clear on your expectations and avoiding ambiguity will all help you. Focus on Future You communication and anticipate success. Being a clear, unambiguous communicator saves time and energy and is key to helping your team thrive. In the next chapter we will look at other ways you can enable your team to do their best work. First, your key takeaways.

Key takeaways

- Ambiguity is the enemy of good communication. When in doubt, double-click.

- Trust can be built or broken through communication.

- Good listening is a brain-friendly way to build trust. The more you can do that, the braver, bolder and more honest everybody will be.

- Nobody sees your good intentions. They only experience the impact your actions have on them.

- Assume positive intent – most people want to do a good job. Be curious, not furious.

- Notice and question your filters and biases.

15
Enabling A 'Future You' Team

Two items appear on the Future You wish list of almost every leader I work with:

1. Quality time to do more of what is important

2. A competent, motivated, engaged, happy, accountable and proactive Future You-orientated team

If you've read and completed the activities to this point, you probably have much more of the first than you did when you began. The second activity takes longer. It requires that you become more of an enabler of others than a fixer of everything, learning to delegate to and rely on your team and help them to thrive, too. This chapter will help you to cultivate a team with a Future You approach.

Motivation

I'm often asked how to motivate people, and my answer is always the same: *Ask them*.

'More money' is not a motivator for everyone. Nor is beer on tap or regular team dinners. While one person is hugely motivated by a big bonus, another would prefer flexible work hours that fit in with term time. Another wants a clear development plan to work towards a qualification or promotion. Another wants to do compressed hours.

As their leader, your job is to provide a great environment, recognition, flexibility, purposeful work and support. But people have to take responsibility for their lives and their careers too. Focus on what you can influence and change and help them do the same.

> 🔆 **ACTIVITY 44: Motivation – Team exercise**
>
> Write the word 'motivation' on a whiteboard or flipchart and ask team members to write on Post-It notes all the words or phrases they associate with that word. Add all the Post-Its to the board and you'll get all sorts of insights about what motivates your team. Further discussions can include looking at how they might get more of what motivates them and less of what doesn't (always keeping in mind to focus on what you can influence and change).

Time to stop fixing!

Many of the clients I work with recognise that they are still too 'operational' and less strategic than they need to be. They're so used to fixing everything, it's become their default position. If you're in fixer mode too, you're probably diving into your emails first thing and getting too many 'have you got a minute' interruptions. This means you're reacting to events rather than focusing on the most strategically important ones. When you're trapped in the vicious circle of busyness, it may seem quicker to tell people what to do or do it yourself – and you may be right in the short term. The problem with this approach is that it reinforces dependency and denies your team the chance to work things out for themselves. Why would they, when they know you'll 'sort it out'? This means you're permanently on the back foot.

People flourish when they are able to generate solutions and take responsibility for their decisions and actions – assuming that you've got their back and they feel psychologically safe to ask for guidance, speak up, make mistakes and learn from them. If this 'fixing' sounds familiar, you are not alone. And if you truly want to change this, it's time to focus on the Future You thoughts that will get you there. Take some time out to do just that, if you haven't done so already.

Delegation

If you are to successfully do your job, you will need to ensure that your team takes responsibility, too. Great delegation will get you more quality time *and* build the competent and confident Future You team you need. My delegation checklist in the resource library (www. effortlessleaders.com/lynn-scott-leader-unlocked) lays out the process and describes how to avoid the common pitfalls. Start by choosing one person you trust and delegating one thing at a time to them. Be clear about your expectations, the end in mind, deadlines and definition of success. When you delegate tasks, focus on what you can influence or change, and help them do the same. Delegate more tasks to more people as you grow more confident and comfortable.

This shift may take time if your team is used to command-and-control or micromanaged leadership. Your team may continue to ask you for instruction or copy you in on emails to cover their backsides, but Future You is more 'enabler' than 'fixer'. You free up time and energy when you pass more decisions *down* the line – with clear expectations and accountability – rather than *up* the line. When you say, 'Copy me in if it's a decision that *only* I can make', you free your brain for the work only you can do and show you trust your team to do the right thing.

This does not mean you'll never need to advise, fix or instruct. There's a time for instruction, when there's only one correct way to do something, you're explaining a new task from scratch or the situation is urgent – but those times are rare. Most of the time, it's better to enable, empower and encourage others to grow their skills, confidence and critical thinking. Think of it as creating the leaders of the future. Remember your pause button when you're tempted to dive in and fix things.

ARE YOU A FIXER OR AN ENABLER?

Fixer to enabler

WATERS: Let it flow

The best enabling conversations flow like water. WATERS is a conversational framework I designed to simplify enabling individuals and teams. In WATERS, we start with the end in mind, anticipate success, allow time for exploration, make decisions, recognise choices and options and agree on actions together. Once you're familiar with the model, I'll show you how to use it in one of 'those' conversations – you know, the ones you dread – and give you some practical strategies to prepare for those conversations. You'll find the WATERS framework as a download in the resource library (www.effortlessleaders.com/lynn-scott-leader-unlocked).

The WATERS framework

What and why: Be clear on what you want to achieve in this conversation. What's the end goal?

Anticipate success: Anticipate success as you start the conversation. What steps can you take to make the conversation a success?

Tell me more: Using deep listening, let the other person describe the current situation. What's happening now? What are the key issues, opportunities or challenges? Explore what-ifs, challenge either/or thinking and any 'shoulds', separating thoughts from facts.

Evaluate: Consider possible solutions or potential courses of action. What options are available to you? What are the pros, cons, costs and consequences of each?

Result: Decide what each of you will do now to get the result you want, and when it will be complete. Let your team member take the lead

Support: Ask your team member what support they need from you or someone else. Make sure that requests are clear and unambiguous.

The model is not necessarily linear; you may jump back and forth between steps a few times. This is fine, if you are making progress. Below is an example of a short water cooler conversation using the WATERS model.

> **Team member (TM):** Have you got a minute?
>
> **You:** I've got ten minutes. What do you need? (W) [*Note:* Manage your time boundary. Anticipate success (A) always.]
>
> **TM:** I need to know how to approach Dave about year-end.
>
> **You:** Tell me more – what do you need from me to help you do that? (T) [Note: Ask, don't tell.]
>
> **TM:** I need to know what to do.
>
> **You:** Where are you up to with year-end? (T) [*Note:* Ask, don't get sucked into telling him.]
>
> **TM:** I'm a bit behind. Dave's not happy.
>
> **You:** How might you deal with this, then? Any ideas? (E) [*Note:* Let him think this through. Pause button time.]
>
> **TM:** I've no idea.

You: What have you considered so far? (E)
[*Note:* Keep asking.]

TM: Hmm. I thought about sending Sue to the update meeting to get this done.

You: OK. Anything else? (E) [*Note:* Keep asking. Leave space for him to say more.]

TM: No, I think that'll do it. I'll let Dave and Sue know what's happening.

You: Great. Sounds like you've got it sorted. Anything else you want to do? (R) [*Note:* That wasn't too hard, was it?]

TM: Yes. I'll go and do it.

You: Sounds good. Anything else you need from me? (S) [*Note:* 'Anything else?' is a good check-in question.]

TM: I want to look again at how we manage our workload at year-end.

You: OK – bring some ideas to our next one-on-one. (E) [*Note:* Let him come to you with his ideas first.]

Remember, the better the questions you ask, the better responses you'll get. A good question is anything that helps the other person think productively, anticipate success or generate ideas and solutions. Avoid leading questions like 'Have you thought about...?' whose subtext is 'I think you should'. These types of questions do not encourage people to think independently. You should also ask only one question at a time, rather than 'question stacking', because the other person won't know which question to answer first. If you get stuck, 'What else?' is a great way to keep momentum going. Ask, then shut up. When you listen well, your questions will flow naturally. Keep in mind that silence after a question often means people are reflecting and thinking about their answers. Don't interrupt their flow.

Confident, not difficult, conversations

Even when we're confident communicators, there are conversations we don't want to have. The topic of difficult conversations comes up repeatedly in my coaching work, and I always start by pushing back on the word 'difficult'. If you think a conversation will be difficult, you create a self-fulfilling prophecy. Instead, let's reframe that difficult conversation as a confident or a purposeful conversation. (You'll find my sample scripts for confident conversations in the resource library at www.effortlessleaders.com/lynn-scott-leader-unlocked.) *This conversation will be difficult* is not an anticipate-success thought. *This conversation will help us get to something better* is an anticipate-success thought.

So-called 'difficult' conversations fill us with dread because doing something that feels emotionally threatening triggers our flight-flight-freeze-appease response. Often, we avoid these types of conversations by:

- Hoping things will sort themselves out

- Catastrophising about how the conversation will go until it becomes an enormous monster

- Tackling the conversation without preparation and regretting it

- Trying to soften the blow by wrapping our message in so much cotton wool that it gets lost

- Putting out a passive-aggressive 'general message' to everyone, hoping the person concerned will take the hint (they won't)

If you've ever avoided one of those conversations (haven't we all?), you'll know this has costs and consequences. There's the emotional cost of worrying about it but not addressing it. The lack of productivity or effectiveness because there's something you're not dealing with, and the terrible decisions made because you didn't share your concerns early on. Then there's the frustration your team or others feel because there's something you're not facing. Not to mention your cold sweat at 3am as you worry about what you might say.

Avoid 'piggy in the middle'

Though it's crucial to address niggly issues or conflicts at work, don't be tempted to be the go-between when team members are at odds. You're not Mum or Dad mediating between two squabbling children, so don't offer to speak to one team member on behalf of another. When somebody comes to you about an issue with somebody else, your response should be, 'How can I help you have that conversation with them?' The end.

Replacing hot thoughts

Future You has these conversations with purpose, clarity, honesty and compassion. That is only possible with mindful preparation. When facing 'difficult' conversations, some hot thoughts might pop into your mind. This list shows some common hot thoughts, along with more constructive, empowering Future You strategies to use instead:

1. **Hot thought:** What if the other person cries?

   Better: If they cry, I'll have a box of tissues ready. I'll pause if emotions run high, and we can take a break if necessary.

2. **Hot thought:** I can't find the right words.

   Better: I'll plan some of what I will say and practise it out loud to ground myself, build my confidence and think about language.

3. **Hot thought:** It went badly last time.

   Better: I learned loads from what didn't go well last time and now have better strategies.

4. **Hot thought:** They'll make excuses.

   Better: I need to be more transparent about the consequences of not changing or performing.

5. **Hot thought:** I'm just no good at this.

   Better: I can improve by preparing, trying my best and learning from my mistakes.

6. **Hot thought:** If I rock the boat, things might get worse.

   Better: 'Rocking the boat' is actually bringing a problem into the open to find a better way forward.

7. **Hot thought:** I hate upsetting people.

   Better: I can be compassionate and allow plenty of time for the conversation, even though the message might be hard to hear. This is the best decision for the business, and I will focus on that.

The following table breaks down how to use the WATERS framework to turn 'difficult' conversations into confident ones. You can apply this framework to a wide variety of conversations and adapt it to your needs.

Using WATERS for confident conversations

WATERS	Openers	Questions	Tips
What and why	We're having this conversation because... or This is how I see the situation.	What would you like to achieve at the end? or What is your desired outcome?	Make the conversation about what you *want*, not what you *don't* want. Practise a few times so your message is clear.
Anticipate success	I'm looking forward to finding some great solutions/ ideas.	How can we set this conversation up for success?	This step gets you both thinking about success, setting the tone. Aim for mutual success if you can.
Tell me more	Tell me how you see the situation.	Can you tell me more?	Remember, your reality, their reality and 'objective' reality, all of which are valid perspectives. Seek first to understand. Don't rush this exploration stage.
Evaluate	Let's look at some possible solutions.	How do you see Option A working? Option B? What other solutions or ideas do you have?	You've learned from what already happened, so this step is about moving on to what happens next. If there is only one option, say so.

(Continued)

WATERS	Openers	Questions	Tips
Result	Let's map out where we go from here (timescales, actions, results).	What is your first step? When and how are you going to do it?	Don't summarise the other person's next actions for them. Let them do it. Avoid asking, 'Does that make sense?' 'Double-click' on vague statements, such as 'I'll do it ASAP'. No ambiguity allowed.
Support	Tell me what you need from me to help you progress or succeed.	Who else can contribute?	Ask them to be clear on the specific support they want from you. Support is *not* doing the work for them, being a go-between or letting them off the hook.

Once you've used this framework a few times, you'll notice how much more easily these kinds of conversations flow. You can use WATERS for quick catch-ups, personal development conversations, one-on-ones and, of course, coaching conversations. Enabling your team happens one conversation at a time.

Building your team

Imagine asking everybody in your team the question I asked you right at the beginning (and which we'll come back to shortly): 'What has changed for the better in the past six months?' Imagine enabling everyone on your team daily to visualise, imagine and get closer to their future selves. Imagine enabling every team member to recognise the thoughts that lead to success and those that keep them stuck. Imagine if everyone on your team started their day by anticipating success and preparing for it.

You can create this Future You team. It's the kind of team that we all dream of, that we all want to lead or be part of. A Future You team is a confident, high-performing and energised team that has purposeful, honest conversations. It has influence and impact and it has abandoned busy-being-busy culture. A Future You team anticipates success in everything it does and is a beacon of light to others.

You can create that team. You have everything you need. You can do this because you anticipate success for yourself and your team every day – and it shows. It's now time to teach what you've learned to your team – start with the end in mind and work from there. Now, for the final time, your key takeaways.

Key takeaways

- Delegating key tasks to your team, with an anticipate-success approach, will give you more quality time to focus on your strategic leadership priorities. It will enable you and them to become more confident and competent.

- If you want to know how to motivate people, ask them.

- The WATERS framework is to help leaders manage goal- or decision-based conversations. WATERS stands for What and why, Anticipate success, Tell me more, Evaluate, Result and Support.

- If you think a conversation will be difficult–it will be. Anticipate a purposeful, confident conversation instead and remember those anticipate-success thoughts.

- If you want your team members to think for themselves, ask more questions, use your pause button and give fewer instructions. This will help each one align with their future selves.

- Everything you've learned in this book can be shared with the team. You can co-create a Future You version of your team and watch it fly!

Summary

Congratulations on finishing this book. If you've done the activities, asked yourself challenging questions, anticipated success, noticed your thoughts and connected and aligned with Future You, you've now honed a great set of strong belief muscles. You are magnificent.

I wrote this book to inspire you to find and tap into your inner wisdom, knowledge and courage in practical ways. It was my goal to help you rise, phoenix-like, from the baggage, beliefs and habits that have weighed you down, zapped your confidence and reduced your impact. You know that your influence and positive impact can shine bright. The brighter they shine, the more you realise they were there all along. Becoming Future You isn't a personality transplant. You're not pretending to be someone you're not, making yourself small or faking anything. You're becoming the best version of yourself, doing your best work with passion and grounded energy. You're becoming the leader everyone wants to work with and for. Do you occasionally experience self-doubt? Of course; you're human. The difference is that now you know doubt is a sign that you're ready for your next iteration of Future You, not a reason to get back in your box.

Let's return to the scenario I gave you at the beginning of the book. Six months from now, you and I are meet for a drink. You say, 'Lynn, I want to tell you about all the great things that have happened since I read your book. I feel like a different leader. So much has changed for the better.'

What will you tell me as we raise a toast to your success? Let me know: email me at lynn@lynnscottcoaching. co.uk. I answer every email (except the spammy ones).

Next Steps

Please help me to spread the word. If you loved the book, please leave a review on Amazon (you can review the book on Amazon even if you bought it elsewhere). Every review helps enormously. Thank you, this means a lot to me.

Work with me

If you want more personalised support to grow your leadership confidence, influence and impact I offer one-on-one executive coaching and intimate, high-end group programmes to senior leaders. I am also available to run bespoke virtual master classes for your group or organisation. For more information, contact pat@lynnscottcoaching.co.uk.

Connect with me

You can also connect with me on LinkedIn by scanning the QR code below or by visiting www.linkedin.com/in/lynn-scott-senior-leader-and-team-coach:

Join my free Facebook community to access training, articles, masterclasses and other leadership resources. Scan the QR code below or visit www.facebook.com/groups/leaderunlocked:

Visit my website: www.lynnscottcoaching.co.uk

To join my mailing list, which includes weekly leadership tips, strategies and ideas, contact pat@lynnscottcoaching.co.uk.

Acknowledgements

To the leaders I've coached over the last twenty-five years, thank you for everything you've taught me.

To my beta readers, Andrea Saunders, Jane Harding, Sam Grayston and Anita Sach – thank you for your guidance, wise counsel, unstinting generosity and honesty.

Thank you to my designer Julie Waring for translating my thoughts into visuals. I hope you love them as much as I do. And to Peter Bluckert who introduced me to the power of coaching more than two decades ago – you changed my life in so many ways.

To Pat for organising my work life brilliantly. I couldn't do without you.

Most of all, to my husband, Brian, my rock.

The Author

Lynn Scott is a global executive coach who helps C-Suite executives and senior leaders build their leadership confidence and impact and achieve better results without working harder or longer. She's an International Coach Federation Master Certified Executive Coach (MCC).

She's a columnist for *Coaching at Work* magazine and a previous Board Director for UK ICF. She cut her leadership teeth in the travel industry where, as head of operations, she led multicultural teams worldwide.

She lives in France with her husband, Brian, and Bowser, the rescue cat.

🌐 www.lynnscottcoaching.co.uk